PRAISE FOR *NO ROOM*

"Spare, fierce and powerful. . . . *No Room* is a revelation. Open to any page and have your breath taken away by this extraordinary writer."

 —JUNOT DÍAZ, author of Pulitzer Prize and National Book Critics Circle Award-winning *The Brief Wondrous Life of Oscar Wao*

"It is a safe hunch that our best critical theology is done in poetic idiom that crosses boundaries, offends niceties, and dares beyond evidence. This collection of poems by Harold Recinos makes that bet a sure thing. Recinos is alert to the lived reality with all of its wounds, hates, and deathliness. He is, moreover, alive to holy force that surges among us. Best of all he is alive to the capacity of rhetoric to probe the depths of systemic violence to hope in honesty that denies nothing."

 —WALTER BRUEGGEMANN, author of *The Prophetic Imagination*

"As the counterpoint to longstanding American silences, the images in Harold Recinos' *No Room* unlock an honest history. Border walls, desert crossings, plagues, and lynching trees—signs of a waning democracy—inundate this collection. Above all, the poems in *No Room* seek justice. Now and again, they also signal renewal, community, and joy."

 —TERESA LONGO, author of *Visible Dissent: Latin American Writers, Small U. S. Presses and Progressive Social Change*

"In this new collection of poems, Harold Recinos reminds us what it means to remember as a means of strengthening our gratitude for the precious gift of life. These poems come as prophetic words always do—to unsettle our complacencies and embolden us to face the indignities of this world with the stronger resolve of compassionate justice. They are the witness of one who dares to dream in the midst of this world's evils, refusing to be silenced by the guardians of the old order of racism and disordered patriotism. They will offend those who insist that faith is simply another form of blind loyalty to the state, but will fortify all who desire to share the poet's dream of a just and merciful world where dignity is a divine birthright given to all, and equality the measure of what democracy is meant to be."

—MARK S. BURROWS, translator, scholar of historical theology, and author of *The Chance of Home: Poems*

No Room

No Room

HAROLD J. RECINOS

RESOURCE *Publications* · Eugene, Oregon

NO ROOM

Copyright © 2020 Harold J. Recinos. All rights reserved. Except for brief quotations in critical publications or reviews, no part of this book may be reproduced in any manner without prior written permission from the publisher. Write: Permissions, Wipf and Stock Publishers, 199 W. 8th Ave., Suite 3, Eugene, OR 97401.

Resource Publications
An Imprint of Wipf and Stock Publishers
199 W. 8th Ave., Suite 3
Eugene, OR 97401

www.wipfandstock.com

PAPERBACK ISBN: 978-1-7252-7024-4
HARDCOVER ISBN: 978-1-7252-7023-7
EBOOK ISBN: 978-1-7252-7025-1

Manufactured in the U.S.A. 07/02/20

CONTENTS

SUNDAY	1
TONIGHT	2
MARTIN	3
WHITE JESUS	4
THE CHOSEN	6
SUGARCANE BOYS	7
RADIATOR	8
FACES	9
HEAVEN	10
THE TEACHER	11
AMERICAN FUNERAL	12
BORDERS	13
PRAYER	14
THE MOURNERS	16
LADY LIBERTY	17
OLD STORY	18
THE COMPOSITION	19
PSALM 96	20
THE INCARNATION	22
MESSAGE	24
LOVE	25
PSALM 137	26
A NEW SONG	27

Contents

WHITE PRIVILEGE	29
THE WALK	31
THE SEASON	32
STAY HERE	34
SKIN	35
NO ROOM	36
SCHOOL DAY	38
THE STORE	39
THE ALTAR	41
WELCOME	43
JIM CROW	44
SOUTH BRONX	45
THE BEDROOM	46
MI BARRIO	48
REVEALED	50
RESTORE US	51
EDGE OF HELL	52
SWEETNESS	54
LULLABY	55
IN THE BEGINNING	57
NUYORICAN	59
STREET VENDOR	60
A DAY	61
THE SLUSH	62
SHADOWS	63
ATATIANA	65
WHITE HOUSE	66
SWEET LOVE	68
WORDS MATTER	69
CONVENIENCE STORE	71

Contents

STARRY NIGHT	73
HERITAGE	74
LAST NIGHT	75
WEST FARMS ROAD	77
PATIENCE	78
THE CLOCK	79
NO LONGER MUTE	80
MODERN TIMES	81
STONE	82
MORNING PRAYER	83
THE CORNER	84
MERCY	85
EXODUS	86
THE PRICE	87
HERE WE STAND	88
PARTNERS	90
PSALM 58	92
SUPREME COURT JUSTICE	94
HEAVEN BELOW	96
GONE	97
VALLEY OF BONES	98
SAND	99
RIVERBANK	102
THE LETTER	103
KREMLIN FB	105
MARCHERS	107
FORGOTTEN HOUR	108
1965	110
THE CLASSROOM	112
BLINK	114

Contents

THANKSGIVING	116
THANKS	117
THE STOOP	119
CLEANING DAY	120
PSALM 46	121
EXODUS	122
REST	124
EL MOZOTE	125
KISSED	126
THIEVES	127
TRAVELERS	129
THE PROJECTS	131
ADVENT	133
THE SEASON	134
THE MANAGER	135
DOUBT	137
THE DISINHERITED	139
WINTER NIGHT	140
JOB	141
SIMPLICITY	142
BRONX TALE	143
LEGAL	145
HATE	146
TRENZAS	147
MIGRANT MOTHERS	149
THE ROAD	150
BLESSING	151
THE CAMPS	152
BARBARISM	153
END OF A YEAR	154

Contents

NEVER FORGETTING	156
SNOWY NIGHT	158
THE *ABUELITA*	159
THE CROSSING	160
THE BEGGAR	161
MEMO FROM GOD	162
THE SIRENS	163
DISJOINTED	164
EARTHQUAKE	165
THE BULB	166
THE INVENTION	167
CAMP HERESY	168
MOUNTAINTOP	169
WHIRLWIND	170
IMPEACH	171
NORTHERN CITY	172
REMEMBER	173
GUATEMALAN BOY	174
THE SEWER	175
PRAYER	177
WITNESS	178
HOLD ON!	179
WAKE	181
MERCY	182
INFANTERIA BOULEVARD	183
HOLLER!	185
THE MAN	186
HERE	187
THE CHILDREN	188

SUNDAY

today we will sit in the
in the little park to talk
about childhood memories
stored in a vast room filled
with detailed books stacked
on strange shelves in us. we
will remember the torn-out
pages, the afternoon stories
of the disappeared, the bitter
knowledge passed around on
the corners of this world, and
the visits to the Cathedral which
was once the church of a martyred
priest where the poor went to find
rest for aching lives for a few
hours on Sunday. we will talk
about impossible things: the
innocent wish, the world that
needs a miracle to help it notice
the voices that haunt us. today,
we will enjoy the park, talking of
Saints visiting us in nightly dreams,
and feeling the breeze softly touch
our Brown faces perfectly made by
a divine hand.

TONIGHT

the evening came quietly
under the streetlights that
played with the voices on
the stoops while skinny kids
ran the sidewalks like birds
scattering in the sky and flying
into light. on the crumbling
windowsills, where flowers
blossomed, old women nursed
fragile beauty as if they were
taken from an ancient Spanish
forest and some divine being
kept watch over them. the
moon in a darkening sky cast
light on Joel's long black hair,
then floating in a gentle breeze,
and in the direction of the small
village she left hundreds of miles
away that has no English name. a
couple of old men sat in front of
Shorty's building watching busses
drive while they talked of love
poems written by Pablo Neruda
in middle age.

MARTIN

still you dream,
a world without
walls, convenient
lies, battering fists,
and pale masks with
hateful grins. still you
dream, freedom for every
race, a dark beloved
Christ offering equality,
peace, justice, and life.
still you dream, *un sueño*,
with the tortured Brown
spics you always welcomed
into a land where their mothers
and fathers, like you, departed too
soon.

WHITE JESUS

you asked me "what does color
have to do with faith?" without
saying a single word about your
White Jesus. the Savior from the
Middle East, the Palestinian Jew,
the unemployed dark man at the
margins, hanging with the wrong
crowd, pursued by cops, rejected
by the powerful, illegally arrested,
tortured, jailed, and lynched on a
tree, who never was a blond-haired,
blue-eyed, love-them-only-in-white
kind of being. you see, this dark-skinned
brother was born to a poor unwed girl
in the stench of a stable, before he said
a first word fled into North Africa
to avoid being killed, grew up wiping
away outcast tears, and hanging finally
from a tree, bleeding to death like a Black
slave who never said Whiteness is pure
and simple divinity. let Jesus be the
color of his skin again, darker than all
your pale dreams and greater than the
white supremacy the West for centuries
attached to him. Jesus was dark like
the night, a foreigner in Europe, a traveler
to America who did not speak English
and the one who still hears the ten

thousand cries of those beaten by
White sin.

THE CHOSEN

you call him president of
a free nation in need of a
Wall. we call him a dictator
with unclean hands who fills
his pockets with the milk and
honey of the land. you call
him the chosen from God up
above. we call him in history,
literature, and art a rosary thief,
fuming dung, a lover of tyrants,
the whore of Babylon, the White
Supremacist Christian poster boy,
and the devil's own kin. you call
him a follower of Christ in a world
of strife. we call him an impertinent
son of a bitch, Jesus' pimp hustling
White Christians for pieces of silver,
smashing the poor, strangers, women,
children, and the global meek with a
barbarous hammer into pieces. you
call him a leader of the free world. we
call him a vain liar, a brazen fraud,
and the most deplorable star-spangled
citizen the world has unfortunately ever
seen.

SUGARCANE BOYS

we talked in the quiet corner
of the block in elegant Spanglish
about the early morning candles
burning in the church, the many
tongues that over the years dragged
themselves with history from other
shores, the extraordinary love two
young men holding hands at the bus
stop shared and God shedding tears
for hypocrites spreading darkness
like it was light. we took a voyage
with words to experience the ocean
winds, reach for the clouds and hear
complete strangers obliterate storms
with happy thoughts. we talked about
the fragile hands of mothers and how
they quietly leave love signs at schools,
in churches, by the grave-plots and
the streets. we talked into the night
like travelers plotting a fresh course
in an uncharted forest, taking the time
to unmask the dreams that slept with
us in the desert.

RADIATOR

the radiator in my childhood
apartment hissed all winter, no
matter the audience. we hung
socks on it to dry to make them,
ready for a new day in school,
and in the kitchen the radio that
only spoke Spanish announced
news about the war in Vietnam,
and the night club featuring the
music of Willie Colon. that old
radiator witnessed the diapers of
three kids, mother's undergarments
laid out to dry, and two decades of
salsa danced in the living room in
dim red light. when the upstairs
neighbors were making too much
noise we banged a hammer on its
upright pipes like it was a marimba
sending a message begging blessed
peace. the radiator in the apartment
was never caged and it still loudly
rings in my ears on cold nights when
curled in bed, thinking about how it
cast Spanglish spells and chanted the
crowded *sofrito* apartment into deep
sleep.

FACES

attacks on poetry
stupidly directed by
academics who see
faces in the clouds
and are too superior
for sweetly imagined
words will always miss
the brilliance of Eliot, the
gifts of Pound, the intelligence
of Angelou, the passion of
Neruda, the theology of
Cardenal, the spirituality
of Thurman, the activism
of Esquivel, the embracing
faith of Auden, the mysticism
of Merton, the rivers of Langston,
and the perfect work of the spirit
in the world's Holy writ! if you
read but a few lines of this poetic
effort and your mind does not bristle
with questions, challenges, and
excitement, well then, what is left
to do but sigh!

HEAVEN

I heard the sound of heaven
coming from up the street like
a steeple church bell wheeled
in a Fifth Avenue parade. I heard
prayers spilling into beautiful
dark flesh that never asked people
living in the tenements to speak
English, change their names, or
run away from the world that never
welcomed them. I heard yelling
from Salvadorans stepping on
nails pushing up from old wood
floors, making Brown feet bleed,
and God relieving them with a kiss
so they would not stagger in the
long day. I listened in the alley to
butterflies fluttering in urban air by
a flowerpot and hearts in the tenement
beating cantos of freedom as grandmothers
planted flowers, corn, and beans on the
fire escape Edens. I felt holiness on one
corner like a strong wind blowing in the
space of a storefront Spanglish revival,
and all this I call home.

THE TEACHER

an English room teacher
asked me in school what
I thought about the poetry
of Langston Hughes. I told
her when the screaming starts
on the streets and people are
running from the popping guns
Hughes makes the world a little
better and the lyrical images in
his words make life by the hour
more bearable. I could see trees,
lawns, kids riding bikes, and flowers
in her suburban eyes right then telling
me she was a long way from the streets
known by the Harlem poet and had
not yet come over to see my bloody
block just up the street from the public
school on East 179th street that does
not have a Spanish name.

AMERICAN FUNERAL

they are changing the record
to impress the country with
brand-name alternative facts,
slicker and quicker than GOP
get-rich schemes. nothing matters
to those conducting the political
heresies of this old-style inquisition
that tortures citizens to confess lies
as truth. the messages of wrecked
history, the dishonored dead, half-light
politicians, and the execution of facts will
count America after this time a modern-
day plague on democracy. we have
watched the wagons circle round the
immoralist too stupid to forget anything
with pounding hearts, witnessed toxic
slop creeping on the border, extorting a
foreign president, rigging elections,
stealing from charities, faking a university,
offending scientists, grabbing them by the
pussy, strutting in the world with cancerous
piety and breaking the law—in the sickest-
ever dream the corrupt politicians and celebrity
lawyers insist the president has done nothing
wrong! shit, bless the hearts of those now getting
rich off the politics at America's funeral!

BORDERS

I crossed the border today
when the impious joined
the president to pray for
a great big Wall and the
Fox News host with the
barrel of a gun said, "Spic,
get out." today, I crossed
the border when every face
on the television screen was
Brown and White *illegal
aliens* roamed the streets, free
to carve their English names
on loathed, dark migrant skin.
today, I crossed the border
in the local restaurant with
the sign saying, "Only English
or you don't get served." today,
I crossed the border when the
church bells began to ring, the
migrants were outside cutting
grass, and God roamed inside a
church overlooking the obscenity
of a country made rich on colored
people's backs.

PRAYER

I said a prayer after the
last urban riots, expecting a
God who stays up nights on
rooftops with junkies to hear
crying, wanting to be heard by
a god who goes hungry in the
apartments, takes beatings like
young mothers, is rushed to the
emergency room with a stab
wound, tells kids when you get
to school eat all you can at free
lunch time, without money for
the subway ride to work and
dying alone in a city hospital
bed. I said a prayer to this Black
fugitive god who knows all about
torture in clandestine jails, girls
raped by gangs in the middle of
the street, jail cells in the northern
cities of the world and the need to
redeem this all-American, English-
speaking hell. I said a prayer in
Spanish in the dawn dim light,
expecting this exiled god to be
wide awake to receive the living
words thrown from the land of the
mutilated, worthless, and near-
dead. I said a prayer to our

undocumented god with bones
that break and flesh that bleeds,
and I waited for sweet hollered
answers.

THE MOURNERS

what if I told you the
mourners gathered in
Lafayette Square dressed
in black with red scarves
to sing old Spanish hymns?
it could be some are young,
with cheeks full of tears
for yet another country
offering them everlasting
grief. what if I told you
they are all in the arms
of God's pity and close
to Jesus who weeps?

LADY LIBERTY

you will not sleep tonight
knowing the lamp beside
the golden door is nearly
doused. the words now read:
"Give me your White-faced
better off, the greedy men
and women who goose-step
piety on the school board,
the government corridors,
the southern border, and
with a sadistic president in
a slave-made and criminal
White House." forget the
wretched refugee from teeming
shores, take the bankers who
make big bucks, the judges
who jail Black and Brown
kids, the white-collar crooks
full of English shit, the cops
who play lawless tricks, and
respectable churches with
people looking away when
pressed. you will not sleep
tonight, unable to breathe free
and gasping with one foot tied
to the old republic's finest and
latest lynching tree.

OLD STORY

close the door softly. don't look back.
what you know on earth is far away in
a different light. you have bits and pieces
of it on the walls of your heart. you feel it
like the damp sand at the Costa del Sol beach
where you tore bread held in your *campesino*
hands. tonight, you will once again hear the
wailing songs rolling out of the dusty mouths
that worked a long time ago in the sugarcane
fields. close the door and sit in the kitchen with
me to practice English. remember home, wrap
it somewhere in your soul, let it say that time is
flat and try like never before to find life in this
place of foreign speech.

THE COMPOSITION

I can hear the weary wails
in the distance like a voice
that whispers in my ear and
see mothers' eyes leaking tears
that drown the earth beneath
their famished bellies. I can see
children's faces in sleep, baby girls
in stained church blankets, people
who have fled pillaged lands and
bloody streets. I raise my eyes with
wretched Mesoamericans to find the
face of God in the heavens and pray
with *campesinos* in open fields for
an end to hate, which they say is the
longest war ever known on earth. in
the name of everything most dear, come
weep with me, say the names of those
for whom I invite you to shed tears, take
into your arms the guiltless pain of
despised human beings from Spanish-
speaking lands and allow the enormity
of love for them to rescue you.

PSALM 96

Lord, tell me things are
not what they seem; let
our cries come into your
ears; do not spend another
second hiding your dark
face; keep the evil men in
politics from mowing down
Brown lives and listen at night
to our fits of howling. Lord,
cast your merciful eyes in
our direction; hand us bread
to eat with your disfigured
dark hands; doom the jailers
on the border; show mercy to
blameless prisoners and set
them free. Lord, tonight let
the words we speak reach
you; look at our faces in the
desert, on the streets, in the
fields, the factories, the strip
malls, detention camps and
slums. Lord, confound
the White House counsels;
put blisters on their tongues;
disrobe the treasonous deceit;
drive them into ruin and let
them wither into dust with
their precious hate. Lord, clear

our hearts of fear; stand with
us on the shores of the wishing
Rio Bravo; judge the White-faced
judges whose teeth drip children's
blood; and repay them the suffering
they enjoy causing. Lord, first and
absolute love, let us find complete
rest with you.

THE INCARNATION

we know a thing or two about
what theologians in high places,
who go round and round in their
world of light, claim an exclusive
right to inscribe. you see, we have
learned more than a few things to
say, walking many years in the dark,
wearing worldly scars handed to us
by people who tried their best in God's
name to beat us into obedience and
have us agree that slavery and poverty
on the earth is a truth conjoined to high
heaven. we know a thing or two about
the claims parceled out in the cogitations
of the divine that do not lift voices from
below and seem always to go out of their
way to make God a sacred White man who
just loves to see us walk around with old-
fashioned chained feet. we know a thing or
two about the Almighty surrendered unto death
whose name we said over many years of hard
work picking coffee, cutting cane, pulling corn,
packing meat, sweeping floors, cleaning toilets,
tending well-to-do kids, planting fruit, and even
building homes for the lynchers who are showered
with pages of White theological blessing! we know
a thing or two about choking on wrong ideas and
fancy words and the everlasting throne defended

by self-congratulating tongues. listen, haughty
theologians and contract intellectuals, with
your ideas so resistant to shame: we are the
dark and repugnant flesh that God on the
earth you walk became.

MESSAGE

she kneels in the wire
cage each night with the
ragged scar on her belly,
calling out a child's sweet
name. her cracked hands
reveal a history of working
in fields, and red eyes in
the cell where she bends
disclose her fight to believe
America is or will again be
a promised land. sometimes
she wakes in that cell in the
dark morning hours, sighing
the old religion here sadly does
not save and the vulgarities
uttered about God in an English
tongue stuns the world God
made from now until kingdom
come.

LOVE

some people say Christianity is
a love story that fell from the sk,
but others in the world only know
hell. the unnamed places of the
dead question this grand tale and
the poor in need of bread insist
prayer and a heavenly idea of
love will never bless a thing.
forgive me for disturbing your
peace with news about the latest
form of misery your country enacts
in the name of a God who delivers
a wilderness of grief to subjugated
places treated to the Whitest divine
blessings. forgive me for asking
why your piety drags women and
children on the border into a brand-
name bog, why the love you claim
comes from God knows nothing at
all of the Bethlehem Star and a whole
lot more of a churchy God? whoever said
congregations are signs of the greatest
love story ever told paid no attention to
the dripping blood of widows, orphans,
and penniless kids.

PSALM 137

by the waters of the Río Grande
we sit and weep when we remember
colonias left behind. on the willows
we hang songs written on carried paper
the border guards and vigilantes in
MAGA hats with long guns mockingly
request, and we cannot find a single
word to croon in this forsaken land. by
the water of the southward-running river
that catches migrant tears, we remember
the gangs slaughtering the innocent in El
Salvador, Guatemala, and Honduras. we
remember murdered and beaten people from
many shores required by torturers to sing.
we remember kids and mothers dashed against
the rocks like the mourning that clings bitterly
now to tongues pressing against the roofs
of mouths. how can we sing the Lord's
harmony in a land where the wicked make us
disappear or offer us poverty, hunger,
thirst, and jail? by the river, we imagine
the glad day the Lord pays back hate and
the new Jerusalem where no one is forced
to walk across deserts, hide from helicopters,
live each day in shadows, or float up, dead, on a
northern shore without tears to weep.

A NEW SONG

lift the voices of the wordless
who sigh, let them speak in the
fields, the streets, the cages, on
all the Walls, and everywhere
against the chastening rod that
makes the weak bleed. let us
rejoice on the stony road North,
lift up the voiceless to the God who
weeps, carry those among us too
frail to walk the flattened paths of
the slaughtered and find along the
way God listening to our cries. let us
shout loud to heaven the dark deeds
done on earth, those prayers to God
drunk on the wine of hatred, the crimes
conducted in the name of God crucified
on earth, the sluggish church without the
flame of liberty and the simple kindness
of love. God, hanging on a humiliating
tree, lift the voiceless that belong to the
meek, keep them in your way today, let
them stand against the bludgeoning sin
of the fully fed, the rich, whose bodies are
never bent and before your gracious throne
of love so bright. God of these sorrowing days,
take us by our dark-skinned hands, break the
bread of life with silenced victims and keep

us with you, splitting the tight chains owned
by those who refuse to cry.

WHITE PRIVILEGE

in my neighborhood, there is no
such thing as White privilege
that has no time to know stories
about the brutal conquests of empire,
the inhumanity of Black bondage,
the systematic land theft from coast
to coast in the name of superiority,
and even ignorance of Lincoln's order
for the hanging death of Dakota Sioux
fighters in the Midwest. on the block,
we carry the lessons of White privilege
in the color of our skin, the texture of
our spic hair, the Black and Brown blood
spilled working in fields, mines, railroads,
factories, villages, towns, and fancy big-
city places that congratulate themselves
on having diversity training for employees
who will never be shot or dragged by a pickup
truck, nor lynched in the dark for the
color of their skin. in my neighborhood,
God is an underprivileged, dark-skinned
spic, practiced in broken-English speech
that schools and the big-steepled churches
say is not good enough every time a divine
utterance offends White power. in my sweet
chocolate neighborhood, where not a single
multimillion-dollar White criminal owns a
tower with an apartment in which to rehearse

the same ol' American racist shit, we are
showered by reminders we don't belong,
they bounce off the cracked tenement walls,
reach into living rooms from television screens,
stare at us from teachers' eyes in public school,
and even make their way into the open air from
fancy church preachers who never admit the good
Lord made every color of skin. in my neighborhood,
there is no such thing as White privilege conducting
a war in the name of pale skin and the criminal White
whips never dare come around to break our beautiful
Black and Brown skin!

THE WALK

where the city lies beneath
tangled clouds, old tenements
lean to one side, and storefront
churches sing until members
stop their worrying, I could see
in the light coming from a library
window simple stories pouring
into the street with an ingenious
language that saves. this is the
last stop in the desert, you see, far
from slavery in Egypt and almost
too dark for the promises of Jesus
to work, but deep down in our bones
we are not tired.

THE SEASON

we have survived all year,
coughing up stories of the
neighborhood patrolled
by dark-painted vehicles
of empire driven by the
uniformed men who bow
down to the gods dressed
in brand-name suits made
overseas. the "Get out!" shouts
playing on the television set
do not stop even when they
are turned off, and in libraries
the thoughts in reasonable
books remain on their musty
shelves, or are gathered up to
be tossed into the swamp by
the well-trained men who love
to cut the throat of Christ to
please the president laughing
in the wings, like hate was not
a sin. I dreamed of church bells
swinging without sound, and
watched from behind polished
glass the autumn wind in a big
hurry to blow through the streets
it never could name. then, with heavy
sighs in the city, enduring a new

season of decay, I, too, hysterically
coughed!

STAY HERE

look down the street
at the grown men on
the corner sharing a
roll of buttered bread,
shining shoes on feet
rushing to work, and
remembering the old
days in southern towns
where Jim Crow broke
lives faster than yesterday
gone. take a seat for a few
hours, hear them say "Black,"
"Brown," and "beautiful" in a
single sentence, while the
the first-class Ortiz funeral
home procession rolls down
the boulevard with a Puerto
Rican boy in a hearse. lean
against the storefront wall
and take a history lesson for
the rest of the day from people
spat in the face, beaten by cops,
killed like Martin and invisible
in the lily-white church. stay
up tonight, recalling all the scars
you saw and faces that never stop
sobbing and take the picture of your
White Jesus down from the wall.

SKIN

the color of my skin
is like an invocation
of roots with a nip of
Spain drowning in a
deep well, magnificent
Africa stunning the gods
from thousands of years
past, and ancient Indians
from red soil ready to chase
darkness from the White
earth. from the middle of
the ocean to way down in
the Latin south, and back
north to Spanish Harlem,
America that in school
and church I write about has
never been White but no
less equal to you fair-skinned
human beings. the blood
of struggle-laden human
beings breathes for me and
with it I call out in the silence
for the justice America prefers
not to give.

NO ROOM

I entered the room with
the small narrow bed in
a corner beside a sink
with dirty soap, not sure
about lying down for a
rest. I could hear words
dashing around in my head
with a bald truth keeping me
sleepless and wondered: "What
kind of disguise would God
use to walk the corridors of
the fleabag hotel without an
address on the street door, and
what homeless kid sheltered
for the night with a head full
of Sunday annoyances and more
dope than God roaming inside
veins would remember mass in
the South Bronx, with altar boys
carrying a processional cross in
dim sanctuary light?" I recalled
testifying in a storefront church
on the block that forgot my name
more times than I could recall once
junkiedom set in my soul and like
my country finally said you don't
belong. I picked up a Gideon Bible
resting on a night table, flipped its

pages, looking for a scripture lesson
that would guarantee laborers just
wages, salvation for Brown junkie
kids, a message to deliver White
lunatics to the George Washington
bridge, and words for the national
leaders who dress in white cloaks they
believed unstained with blood!

SCHOOL DAY

I saw two little girls with
braided, dark hair laughing
on the way to school, talking
in Spanish. tiny birds chirped
alongside of them while the
early morning light rose to
become a new day. I watched
them fall into history as if
their smiles would reveal
all the details of heaven by
the time the Catholic school
assembled. when Sunday
worship in this city sinks
into silence and the wind
pushes the White resentment
of Brown innocence out to
sea, these young American
faces will return home from
school joking about teachers
and priests to light up the hours
with the migrant innocence that
makes a country disfigured
by hate truly more beautiful.

THE STORE

the bodega on the corner
belonged to Joey's mother,
whom everybody thought the
richest woman on the block.
single moms just out of
their teens visited the place
to get thirty-five cents of
gossip and to buy a few things
with pinched bills that passed
through Wall Street banks,
beggar's fingers, and finally
their cracked hands. I recall
the day Shorty was in the back
of the store next to the candles
with the images of the Holy
Mother, preparing to forge a
note to the local priest, waiting
for him up the street to offer
religious instruction. Shorty
whispered to me that he sees
more lessons on the faces in
the store than a White-faced
God who hangs in church that
never lived in an apartment, went
hungry like him, or came home
with welts on his face from a cop
beating. "Yup," I said. God in pretty
White skin had abandoned the Puerto

Rican tenements, the Spanish-speaking
factories on Bruckner Boulevard, and
all the Spanglish kids who weep for
the crucified Christ beneath the New
York sky.

THE ALTAR

the altar is splintered
though it still holds

your peace and not
a single mystery of

faith is sullied by
it, Lord. the world

nagging in us kneels
in the dim sanctuary

with the ceiling fans
humming to call us

from silent prayer.
Lord, in the early

fall chill we say the
rosary beside watchful

carved Saints' eyes
until our hearts, with

earthly unrest, grow
warm, Lord, before

departing we will light
candles on a stand in

front of Mother Mary,
whom the widows say

will carry us to your
faraway heaven.

WELCOME

early in the morning, when
the world begins in Emilia's
kitchen, two little girls come
to table for tortillas with beans
and instructions about how to
live in a new day like human
beings. the cramped kitchen
table has been a place of prayer,
laughter, sadness, and a sanctuary
for dreams. through its southern
window news by the hour floats
in like voices remembering the
time nothing was between them
like a border. they chant about the
cruelty of daylight for evacuees,
the long walk with blistered feet,
questions about the tenderness of
Christ, the children too tired to hear
mothers speak, the river still crying
on Emilia's face, the strangers too
scared to speak out and their new
world offering little to believe. after
breakfast, on the way to school, the
girls, beautiful like the brown earth,
are told by their mother, "Remember,
America is not foreign land but the
north side of paradise you now call
home."

JIM CROW

on the American side of
the border, in filthy camps,
there is Spanish weeping,
with enough tears to bathe
American churches going
out of their way to forget
God so they can cling to sin.
on the north side of the border
their documented White Christ
does not move stone hearts to
feel migrant pain, to provide
simple aid, to keep us from
the White man's well-practiced,
torturing hands. the Methodist
church, with its well-paid, big-
steepled preachers, does not have
the heart, you see, to work with
Brown people. you can imagine
how the sweet Brown Lady of
Sorrows sobs in the new Jim Crow
camps. listen, in the wicked cages
of a failing White Nation some like to say
God chose the president and you can
hear foul bells ringing in places of
worshipthat cheer the news with
bread and wine.

SOUTH BRONX

home is a foreign country
in a borough of New York
to me. it exists in my air,
the nightmares prowling the
streets, the screams of the
border-caged children, every
time cops take shots at Black
and Brown kids, the countless
days White privileged citizens
deny we made this country great
from sea to fucken sea! my
home is full of dreams made
of a bright light that wakes
me nights with questions tossed
to the fifth floor from the corner,
and my pillow is soaked by furious
tears caused by the country that
denies her Spanish past, the sites
where Indians were tossed in graves,
and the places Africans were kept
in chains. "Promised land, my ass,"
say dark-skinned citizens living
on the block who are detested by
the men who dress up in vile white
sheets and the good citizens using
educated words to hide their hate
for Black humanity, wetbacks,
and spics.

THE BEDROOM

in the two-bedroom
apartment that owned
their lives in a northern
city they covered a brand-
new sofa with see-through
plastic slip covers where it
sat in front of a television
with a hanger for an antenna
and next to a thrift store record
player for little Anthony and
Cheo Feliciano tunes. late nights,
roaches in the dark congregated
in the bathroom, speaking English
about scouting out the kitchen
for scraps. one crowded room,
with two young mothers sleeping
next to their American-born kids,
found Spanish dreams thinking
of things in the apartment that
was a new home. just before the
alarm clock rang you could hear them
sighing for the old country and talking
about the border crossing from Mexico
and the sight of heavy boots on patrol
flying the red, white, and blue to scare
them. soon, they will be getting the
kids ready to attend a school that will
beat them with White history and test

them about its heroes in ways that will
assure them beneath God's sky their
Spanglish lives will not find heaven
on earth.

MI BARRIO

on the dirty broken streets
of this city where the *barrio*
exists, with everything made
from the things we have lost
and are often washed with,
Spanish tears mothers have
come to make a new life. they
learned the colors of autumn leaves,
bowing their heads in the little
park with old women in prayer.
they sat on tenement stoops to
catch first snowflakes on their
Latina tongues and the cheeks
of their beautiful Brown faces
with smiles. the tenements are
home for them, the people always
short on money neighbors, and
some nights the beggars shouting
on Southern Boulevard make more
sense to them than finely dressed
penitents practicing versions of
look-at-me religion. where they
live people still sit on the stoop into
the early morning hours to look at
the stars that watched them begin a
blistering long walk and have children
in the city hospital named to honor
the first republican president. in

their world, overlooked by travel books and beaten down by white-collar criminal politicians, María, Emilia, Ana, Esperanza, Caridad, and even three-legged dogs roam on the side streets to quote bits of scripture and speak their truth without permission.

REVEALED

the new week began
with hundreds of lies
and shared presidential
tweets never close to
the truth. the lawyers
make the rounds on
news shows, denying
what they know: truth
lurks in the dark corner
of the president's head,
yet the man can only
say not a single drop
of love is left for the
aching world. in these
times, truth is a sign
in a failing democracy
about nothing left to
believe.

RESTORE US

once upon a time, with sheer
stubbornness we held hands
and made a human chain in front
of the festering big house to stand
in simple witness. we sang old
protest songs in the languages of
two countries that made their way
to heaven and poured tears into
nights like prayer. once upon a time,
candles were held in hands of many
colors in dark churches, in blackened
night where Spanish cries drifted back
across the border, always to brighten
places forgotten with the simple offer
of light. once upon a time, we made
loud noises in front of the first border
Wall, raised and denounced the use of
God's name to pander savage hate for
Brown kin. do you remember?

EDGE OF HELL

how many rivers will the poor
cross today without a body
washed to sea? how many will
gaze at the running waters while
meteors shoot unfettered across
the sky, hankering for home and
a place for new life? when they
speak their first broken English
sentences on the other side, will
northerners be softened by their
accents and see in the busy city
streets, the workplace, the courts,
the jails, the schools, the tenements,
the figure of Christ in his tattered
robes? we never imagined places
across the line no one has actually
seen, and even Ezekiel would have
trouble seeing a wheel way up in the
air and he would not find God near.
hate like swelling wood in the heat
of summer collects crimes by the
hour, laughs at children who cry at
night with us, and makes it easier
to despair. in *barrios*, America is
an arsonist that sets Brown bodies
on fire and looks the other way, and
the burning hollering through a last

breath: you are no city on the hill or
miracle that saves!

SWEETNESS

there are stories here tossed
from windows between the
old buildings like pages of
yesterday's newsprint falling
on a Fourth of July parade. faces
smile when they look out of
windows at the sight of little
girls feeding pigeons leftover
bread. the block shows signs of
fatigue too, like slow-moving traffic
on the East Side Drive and as the
moon rises to give light in the dark,
people talking Spanish go on telling
stories to each other without judgment.
children warm themselves in autumn
air, playing tag and shouting to each
other in Spanglish. the sidewalks have
never been closer to signs of life and
the block that gathers dust blown from
the banks of the East River gets nosier
with the fresh faces of men, women, and
children too dark and more ancient than
this country.

LULLABY

The radiators are humming
tonight, whistling in each
room the same tunes heard
last week, and carrying on
like they are hungry for one
of our plastic plates of rice
and beans. In the alley, rags
worn for work and school
hang from windows, looking
apologetic. The after-midnight
hours like prayer limp in the
apartment and spill into edgy
bodies on second-hand store
beds. We laid quietly with the
radiators like sleep subversives
coughing, then decided to tell
bedtime stories unknown in the
public schools, like wading in
the river when the lights went
out on the other shore and being
very scared, crossing. We talked of
crammed rooms and linoleum
floors, the memories where the
gods breathe and water runs from
faucets to fill glasses with drink.
We never spoke of sheep, did
not let El Cuco spill into our flesh,

and when silence came, wished
for sweet dreams.

IN THE BEGINNING

the last time I saw you
it was nearly winter in
the city where our mothers
dragged their bodies off
to jobs downtown and too
many kids unlike the cold
were vanishing. you joked
about stones blocking the
border entrance, the static
ideas parading inside of the
English-speaking heads about
the Nazareth side of town with
people they said lived without
a past and thick fires already
destroying their futures. Do you
recall the old drunk who was
always on the corner with a pint
of Midnight Express in a brown
paper bag shouting, "Lotería," and
pissing on the fire pump, or the
guitar player we called El Viejo
who sat on the stoop some nights,
clutching an instrument that crossed
an ocean with him, playing for a
crowd of kids? Do you remember
the sound of the tambourine playing
in the storefront church, wondering if
God gave ear to the sweet sounds?

we prayed often with our mothers to
a Savior who never set foot on the block
and until our tongues were too dry to
speak Spanish. it is good to see you
after too many years, and I still have
the imperfect map that led me to other
hapless gardens where I learned Eden,
too, was not to be found.

NUYORICAN

on the corner, a long way
from old San Juan and the
lives hidden by mountains,
Indian, African, and Spanish
blood clings to our flesh and
I declare America will never
erase the scope of this history
reflected in Nuyorican lives. the
star-spangled jail, making our tears
flow to fill more oceans, will never
stop screams from collecting in
heaven, and not a single obituary
from New York will dare to read,
"A Nuyorican never dreamed in
Spanish Harlem of home on the
distant hills by the sea." when we
got birth certificates from the city
where our mothers wept, attended
public schools plodding through
material with not a single Spanish
name, we took our troubles to the
block, unaware God was waiting on
the stoop, calling us with no English
accent by our sweet names.

STREET VENDOR

no one overlooked the old
Puerto Rican lady, with long,
white, braided hair, who climbed
stairs during American holidays
selling *pasteles* for a cheap taste
of heaven. I saw her crying one
day at the front door of the old
building, and wiping tears from
hollow cheeks in front of Shorty's
apartment door on the fifth floor.
I tugged her apron and imagined
her the grandmother I never met
who counted stars, told stories, and
never prayed in English. the kitchen
tables in the apartments held her
secrets on cracked plates and sweet
sentences of thanks came up for the
old woman in the hallway who made
barrio treats with dark hands matching
penny colors in her purse. I can tell you,
whenever this lady peddled her stuff
light gathered in the places we called
home.

A DAY

in the building that replaced
a village in the hills that was
never lost in clouds, nor hidden
by the tall pines that provided
wood for artisan crosses, was
the apartment called home for
two years. a torn Bible collected
dust by the hour next to a cheap
lamp placed on an altar with
ceramic Saints and a faded
picture of a very old couple
on a black sand beach with
bonfire smiles. when the cold
visited the old city, White tourists
went tanning across the border,
ignoring for days the things they
needed to confess. she still hears
the monstrous wailing caused by
the fired guns taking the lives of
the innocent. the gang members
never mourn and church bells
don't ring. when you take time to
have a close look, you notice the
good-bye candles in her eyes the
light avoids due to fear.

THE SLUSH

one cold winter day I found
New York in the bus station,
soaked at the ankles with city
slush, yelling expletives sharp
enough to crumble the walls
and slay rabid dogs. the faces
in the crowd had lives familiar
to the workers in the station, like
old songs, and you could see White
flesh gathering on lines for rides
back to grass-covered land on
the other side of the river. one
cold winter day at the old bus
station the custodians who clean
toilets and mop floors with rough
Black and Brown hands gave me
a tiny bag of dust to toss into the
wind, advising me to make a wish
for fresh dreams.

SHADOWS

we just
arrived
from a
place
hundreds of miles
away
with mourners
marching
for weeks,
with Brown skin
that prayed
long
in the
black nights
against the
party of
White sin.
the
people
sang in
the dark
about
settling
in a
promised land
that
hoarded honey
and

praised the
saccharine piety,
defending
fat, old
men
with filthy
tongues
in power.
they
sang,
"Even God
is a
stranger to
these
incestuous
fucks."

ATATIANA

last night in the city, where
the West begins, I died with
the young Black woman who
was playing a video game at
home with her nephew before
being shot by a White cop. all
night I hollered "Ave Maria" in
the dark, telling our Mother full
of Grace another mindless bullet
from an officer's gun has taken
a precious sister and blameless
heroine of color from this life.
the White cop's shot will last the
eight-year-old boy who lost an
aunt forever, his cracked heart
will sink more into the Whiteness
of America, where Black, Brown,
Yellow, and Red humanity weeps
for the history of bloodshed. I am
murdered with this Black humanity,
injured with nephews, sobbing sisters,
the good-bye parents, relatives, and
friends, the city kids killed by errant
cops, and the trampled of the earth. I
am a son of an exiled Indian with a
Black Puerto Rican soul who weeps
and promises never to forget the name
of another innocent dead: Atatiana!

WHITE HOUSE

the White House is the
home of a wicked man
who makes the poor weep.
he jokes about the sound of
nails driven into flesh and
with his evangelical assassins
gives thanks to a perverse God,
delivering hunger, thirst, torture,
and death to the weak like fresh
bread. the White House is where
you find the man theological idiots
claim is the chosen one of God,
and each day they are thankful the
president's torpid brain and feet
tramples decency to bits and stomps
life right out of the dark-skinned. the
White House, the imprudent preachers
claim, is hitched to divine truth, though
the hush money john is loose with truth
and does not know in the beginning
was the Word, and that Word is not
him. every day the poor crowd into
his camps, gather outside his home, and
wait for the coming day when rats will
pick away at his bones. one day, the
White House will no longer be home
for this criminal imp, the devil will
take the wicked man with all his friends

to a fiery pit, and we will shout, "Hosanna in high heaven, the Lord is near!"

SWEET LOVE

most of all I love the birds,
awake with morning songs
in the rising Mesoamerican
Sun, the sound of the hungry
children making their lives
with laughter, the old women
who say exaggerated prayers
before heading to the market,
the daily discovery of fresh
mysteries. I love the night you
told me God has a Brown face
and speaks Spanish with a soft
voice, always sings a little off
pitch, and lifts water and honey
to your lips. I cherish how you
said not a day disturbed by death,
nor stubborn worldly madness
on the warring streets, could keep
life and love from persevering in
you. I must tell you the keepers
of fear will never reach me here
with you waiting for exquisite
light.

WORDS MATTER

maybe I forgot your voice
for a little while, sitting here
on this roof far from the clouds
that cover the mountain where
your village sits. newspapers
in the city will never talk about
the scent of flowers arising from
your hair, the reddish sky nearly
writing your name, and falcons
perched on high peaks swooping
down to greet you. I still hear
the angels that cried out the day
we scaled the mountainside for
the first time imagining riches
at the summit and God's trumpets
welcoming us. a civil war raged
in the valley beneath us like last
days, yet we found time to smile
despite the world weeping. my
favorite poet, Auden, lived for a
time on the Lower East Side of
Manhattan in a building a block
away from me and he thought
poetry hardly changes the world,
or perhaps it only enforces a set of
opinions on the left or right! but I
disagree. Words alone matter, and
you, sweet Brown woman, caressed

by the Word made flesh, bear witness
to the greatest poem: Eden will not
perish in this fatally divided world.

CONVENIENCE STORE

the single light over
the door of the 7-Eleven
shines on the wrinkled
faces of the Spanish-
speaking men standing
in the lot as a gust of
wind blows dead leaves
to the other side of the
street. you may not believe it
but these migrant men
mentioned in the daily news
reports that know a great
deal about tilling the earth
hide in the shadows when
the light of a new day comes.
 they are talking in low
voices while citizen bums
visit the convenience store for
a beer. these migrant laborers
do not expect heaven to send
aid through parting clouds
to them. they simply wait for
a boss to offer work for Xavier,
Julio, Diego, Ramón, Jesús, Edwin,
Goyo, Ramiro, Elías, and broken-
English Sam. one guy out loud
reminds everyone that 7-Eleven

never closes and after a silence
he remarks, "*Pero* America, *coño*
wants to build a Wall. *Mierda!*"

STARRY NIGHT

I live in the city where buildings crumble when church bells ring, prayers explode every night from the mouths of frail single mothers, and the little kids wonder what the next day will bring. I live in the city where theology fails to offer words to fill sadness, where language rushes to speak of survivors on the street and the Spanglish people who change into clean clothes to keep from staining pious pews still deliver nothing. I live in the city that belongs to the unknown people called spics, slapped around by a nation full of hate, complete with chilling screams. I live in the city that searches in the dark for unknown gods to experience the simplest touch of paradise and the fragile delights of love.

HERITAGE

I found my *sofrito* self
in the smell of beans
cooking beside white
rice, speaking truth to
my Puerto Rican Taino,
African, and Iberian skin.
I saw my Nuyorican face
in the clouds that passed
over the roof after floating
here from the Americas to
say *bendicion*! I look out
the old tenement window
and feel flooded by names,
ancient secrets, and songs
in a language of their own
that I understand, and the word
vaya gives me yet another
animated night full of sweet
life!

LAST NIGHT

we have arrived in the city,
wanting very little from the
country that invents identities
for us. God almost died when
we slept in a cardboard box one
afternoon on the Mexican side of
the border, waiting for nightfall,
holding hands. we crossed, hearing
voices singing unfamiliar melodies
far on the other side, and with Spanish-
speaking affliction made it to this old
city that nightly ferries unkind news
reports about us. the old tenements
here never split dreams, and I swear
they think we belong like altars are
expected in church, the clarity of the
Saints in heaven, and the thirst quenched
in old rooms. for the sake of honesty,
tell them our dark bodies will not steal
a single word of English or expect confessions
from them, but will remind them that despite
all the empty gospel messages thrown
into the American wind, we were here
from the beginning like the patches of
stars in the sky. do not let your hateful
speech get in the way for we come asking
little more than work, bread, home, a school

for our kids, and an end to your stinging
scornful whips.

WEST FARMS ROAD

despite the long nights
in overcrowded rooms
with others innocent of
transgression, and with too
many days carrying a cross
on our dark-skinned backs
on downtown streets, we feel
the rebel piety prohibited by
the pretty White church on Park
Avenue and no one doubts being
nearer to the place God's will gets
done than the Methodist pastor
with his educated speech. we are
Spanish-speaking strangers, crying
in the dark, imploring Americans
not to treat us like scum. we who
are welcomed across the border by
an undocumented God, sit in apartments
that first appeared in dreams with old
women humming hymns and street
preachers heard outside shouting on
with dust on their tongues, "The world
is good news without end."

PATIENCE

at the break of day
the people chant in the
storefront church with a
chill wind blowing through
the front door that still has
a barbershop sign on it and a
young boy inside thinks Christ
is too late and maybe too frail
to walk too far. when the morning
hollers end, their hearts will turn
back into stone for the length of
a new workday in places around
town and every one of these Brown
faces will look for a road, maybe
even a subway ride, leading to the
streets of Bethlehem that are open
to Spanish accents and indifferent
to the color of skin.

THE CLOCK

the clock wound for work,
once for life, hiding nothing
from the minutes, waiting for
words to enter open air, talked
up in thick books making them
strike true, chimes equally for
every one of us. it calls to us in
the morning, counts strokes for us
at night, and untiringly it ticks,
like in the beginning. the holy
cannot escape its loud alarm,
its merciless taking of life by surprise,
and the questions it brings to
the mind of gods so noticeably lost
while talked about on earth.

NO LONGER MUTE

in the dimming light
where it feels in the
latest American hour
like disbelief, we can
consider the value of
truth more important
than a president naked
and exposed. God is
least to blame for the
imbecile in office, his
deep regard for cruelty,
and his perilous sack of
lies. we, the citizens
witnesses to the
insanity and twisted
acts of State, are called
upon to act.

MODERN TIMES

the 22 people killed in
El Paso for having Brown-
colored skin was the latest
reminder of Anglo lynch
mobs hanging Mexicans on
trees and the need again for
colleges, cities, churches,
and synagogues in America
to spirit Brown refugee bodies
across the southern border in
the name of the tortured and
rejected Brown-skinned and
non-American Christ, who smiles
when government thugs and
vigilante citizens simply cannot
find them. the fools. they don't
even know *vigilante* is a Spanish
word that migrated into their
tongue.

STONE

the gods have been named
on many shores in different
tongues, talked about until
their advocates on earth
had nothing left to say and
stuffed in distant corners by
the wounded who dared sip
their sacred drink and mention
them by name. the gods have
not prohibited evil men from
doing what they wish, like slaughtering
children in daylight with soldiers
trained by Christians, killing priests
who implored the world for peace,
and scattering the bones of the innocent
on the hillsides by the places where
the spiritually decadent gather to sing
hymns. the gods also find their way
into sweetgrass, incense, and the smoke
rising from the ashes of those who said
their prayers. so, here with fear and
trembling, in us there is no hurry to
find shelter in a nearby church or gather
with those who have drawn swords and
speak with twisted tongues quite divinely
of evil things.

MORNING PRAYER

I sit quietly in the fading dark, examining a wordlessly unfolding new day. suddenly, children begin making loud speeches on the sidewalk and aging couples with trembling hearts are seen walking. this morning I must confess not knowing anything about this America, waking up now to shove itself into our faces like flies in a field of unpleasant things we brush away. I feel a prayer dragging its heels from a dark corner inside of me, almost afraid of those who rip out the tongues of strangers, and it says, "Lord, renew hope and welcome dark bodies into this land."

THE CORNER

the clock in the quiet
hours of the morning
asks the kids on the
corner whose mothers
are scarred by hard
work about their nods
made possible by a
fix from a fresh bag
of dope. the Puerto Rican
boys, who are fixtures on
the corner, know every
Spanish word in their
mothers' fleshy hearts,
and now they recall, in
the spaces where they do
not nod out, stories from
Sunday school, rewritten
to say, "In the beginning
was the end, and heaven
did not weep!"

MERCY

on the dirty sidewalk where
hope stands in wait with us
and church bells ring news of
God, the mystics can never
be talked about with the kind
of certainty the pastors fondly
preach. standing in front of the
Perez grocery store you can hear
a different story when fire trucks
rush across the avenue, and Tito,
who just got out of jail on Riker's
Island, yells, "The block is not under
God's sentence of love." on the corner,
where nightmares are equally
distributed, people say, "The Bible
should have written, 'the rich you
will always have with you and
the testimony of the dead poor
gone forever from this world
leaves the hopeless ministers and
their stiff flocks bearing witness
to cold hearts.'" on the corner, there
is no good time to make us stand
in the mystic moment in wait, and
the chains the country placed on
our wrists will never utter a single
Klan objection!

EXODUS

the miracle in Egypt for
the enslaved children of
Israel is carried in a tattered
pocket from the moaning
fields down south. in the
Bronx, to this very day we
reach in to feel the sand on
which slavers walked and
touch the end of servitude
that left Pharaoh trampled
beneath servants' feet. today,
our screams still rise to the
highest heaven, to God who
delivers, who walks across
boundaries, a pillar of fire and
mighty cloud. tonight, on the
Black- and Brown-despised
streets, hollering belief with
a moon leaking light through
a clouded sky, we carry in pockets
and bags the promise of God's
blessing, and step by step, with
eyes on the prize, make our way
to freedom.

THE PRICE

we look up at the sky under
which life began in another
country, smiling at the round
face of the moon peeking over
the rooftops to see the earth
Brown faces that were welcomed
into the world by mothers who
struggled and labored to give
life. we remember the last
prayers peddled in the middle
of the night until it was time to
creep away from the mysteries
of the village, and how we called
upon the Holy One with piercing
Spanish petitions to escort us into
the wilderness and rain down bits
of *manna* for us to eat on the long
journey. we have been in this new
city, unfolding life like an old map,
some nights hearing in the wind the
grandmothers, who like Rachel weep
for us. after walking three thousand
miles in four months, we expect to
start life over again by the waters of
the East River of Spanish Harlem.

HERE WE STAND

I worked in the sugarcane
fields for hundreds of years,
with a back bent and scarred
from a White whip swung by
a laughing Spanish face that
was only pleased when slaves'
and laborers' heads bowed. I
was determined to sing, dance,
and breathe free on this land
that never mourned the death
of people with dark skin who
made it rich. I prayed when you
called me a filthy, good for
nothing spic, then I suffered in
the days you denied my people
work, school, food, and a place
in your lily-white world. from
Puerto Rico to New York, El
Salvador to DC, México City
to LA, you tried to keep us down,
saying, "This country does not sing
with greasers and spics, this land
tis not of thee nor will the old rich
men with calloused hearts who rob
it clean ever set you free." you can
spit on me until your mouths run
dry in all the cities made on murdered
Indian lands and by slaves you never

wished free, but the great God who sent
a Savior, vilified by a terrorist State and
official piety until hung on a lynching
tree while his mother cried at his feet,
will bring righteousness and freedom
to despised people.

PARTNERS

the children in the camps
speak another language
in hateful America, separated
without explanation from
mothers, never treated like
human beings, abused by
the unspeakable acts of men
standing guard and disregarding
their screams. in spite of the
national illness, the citizens of
my country gladly attend church
to wait for the next hymn, and
they walk right by jailers' doors,
not denouncing the White doctrine
taking toddlers' lives in American-
made cages shaking with loud cries.
the hollering will never fade as time
moves on, it will learn to speak English,
deluge the history books, be seen in
photos hanging in museums and images
on film. these children you see will one
day be witnesses, they will talk about
being snatched from mothers and the
death tolls in America's camps. these
children whose lives mean nothing will
write American history to tell the world
about the accomplices of evil who loved

to pray in public and not say a damn thing.

PSALM 58

let us believe God
is not content with
the country and can
use more than a little
recognition from the
savage dispositions
in citizens who like to
dress with a flag. let
us at the height of all
despair cry to heaven,
certain bruised bodies
can dance away hours
of sadness inflicted by
lawmakers with truant
faith. let us confess the
day is coming when the
blind will see, the deaf
hear, and the wretched
in America will get the
clearest view of your
accepting face. let us,
on this most precious of
all days, trust that heaven
will dispatch judgment
for those with poisoned
tongues and the vain old
men who rule the world
by unjust laws. Lord, let

divine vengeance deliver
us from sin to a sweeter
life!

SUPREME COURT JUSTICE

a middle-aged Puerto Rican
man is standing in the middle
of the block wearing a t-shirt
that reads: "Sonia Sotomayor,
the Nuyorican Supreme Court
justice from the housing projects
in the South Bronx—*Vaya!*"
the back of the dingy white shirt
said facts in the news worth
print. a little girl plays on an
empty lot next to an alley where
a dog coughs. a woman looking
out of her window lets long hair
droop on the sill like it was about
to call out a name. a statue of
St. Francis is on a second-floor
fire escape with a couple of
pigeons watching everything
on the street. the oldest beggar
on the block is on the corner by
the Perez Bodega with a paper
cup, collecting petty change and
waiting a little longer for God to
talk to him just like the Holy One
did with Moses when the Torah
descended from the mountaintop.
as the night begins to fall on the
street, a black dressed widow smiles,

waiting at the bus stop when
suddenly a light breeze caresses
her beautiful Brown cheeks.

.

HEAVEN BELOW

the politicians will be left
to themselves by the people
who walked away from the
last candles that burned in
homes in places that never
spoke English. no longer
picking coffee or working
long days in the fields, they
are beginning to look more
like this city. they can still
read time by looking at the
sky, sometimes they wake
up in the middle of the night
with their dreaming full of
trouble and screams. people
who have seen corn grow on
the bones of the dead are learning
to admire the first winter snows, the
sun in the cold, English-saturated
days, and the joys holidays in a
world shadowed by a Wall can
bring. the politicians will be left
to themselves today by these people
whose mouths speak Spanish to the
bitter White crowd saying, "Look, heaven,
like a falling star, is closing in."

GONE

the days are gone when music
played in the record shop
on Tremont Avenue, and the
kids entertained each other
on stoops with stories their
fathers and mothers told from
the old country, and in the storefront
church in the middle of the
block where the Puerto Rican
choir loved doing a Spanish
variation of "Amazing Grace."
the days are gone of listening
to the old women calling up
prayers in front of precious clay
Saints and going with Cuca to
Santería meetings that always
drove Catholic priests mad with
near-dark rooms where Chango
spoke—you know, the Yoruba God
who directed a priestess and was
never testy about speaking South
Bronx Spanish. the days are gone
and still the rich brown sounds of
people coming from all directions
brush their secrets inside of me to
slide me past troubles and to the
alleys where light shines from all
directions.

VALLEY OF BONES

on the southern border, and across America, children are bundled into cages where they make unforgiven history with tears. the suave tormenters in high office who declare soiled lines tell us the world is flat and a big White Wall alone will make the country safe. in the English-speaking churches twisted piety cannot say with gospel certainty that people with beautiful dark skin are children of the God who suffers in every color of human skin. what shall we say to the kids who will struggle all their days to be whole? villains are stone-hearted people with White skin who have yet to find the truth that will set them free? villains are those who always seek to close the mouths of innocent Brown kids who call for mothers too far to hear? surely, it is time to strip away the lies, and for the sake of holy strangers from foreign lands broken by the White House, tell the plain truth!

SAND

in the
desert,
in its endless
drought,
where night
gets cold
and
days
are
bitterly
hot
and
God
can
hardly
do
her
work,
we walk
to
waiting
cities.
in the
desert,
we
carry
dreams
across

its
sand
to places
bottled
water
was
sliced
to pieces
by
racist
hate.
we
whisper
beneath
the stars
the
names
of
villages
into each
other's
ears
on the
way
to
new
cities.
in the
desert,
the

breeze

lets

our

names

ride

in her

arms

all

the way

to

the

waiting

cities

on the

other side.

RIVERBANK

by the ancient river you
know by many names,
that took too many weeks
to reach, the faceless stars
amuse migrants. one night
a ten-year-old boy recalled the
day with violin music rolled up
in a pocket and a fiddle with wear
marks on its neck carried by him in
a cracked black case. he knocked
on a green metal door with one
foot and then stepped slightly back
to wait for an old man named
Ricardo to answer and invite
him in. the music teacher had
a pair of eyes the little boy swore
lighted the darkness in the *barrio*
and they dripped lyrical stories. by
the ancient river that night the boy
hugged his mother, found a spot to
sleep and prayed to get a glimpse of
God's throne when crossing the river
to make his way to New York to play
the violin once again only on sidewalks
and stoops not wet with tears.

THE LETTER

the land
is an
open house,
receiving
unexpected
visitors,
speaking
in
foreign
tongues,
and
hoping
for the
welcome
that
feeds
them
for more
than
just three
days.
the land
is an
open house
that
entertains
angels
with Black

and Brown
faces
from
other worlds,
so
do not
use
thin
faith
to offer
water
to
them
from
dirty
wells.

KREMLIN FB

the department of
provocations made
America its room,
sowing discord on
computer screens
to deliver fake news
and carry a presidential
election to the rich man
in America with a lifetime
of doing wrong things. a
whole flock of so-called
Christians rushed to the
Kremlin rallies pieced
together by hired help
to listen to packaged trash
talk about a Black president
and messages about a brand-
name man elected by God
to take his place from the
Whitest preachers making
a whole bunch of money
from a Reverse Standard
Version book they call
the Bible. Russia was
never any happier than in
this second decade of a new
age, with America divided and
the good book closed to the

cries of marginalized human
beings and the nearly dead. the
Kremlin, sowing discord on the
internet, elected a shitbag president
with no religion and an amoral heart
to the country he never loved and
against a people it wants to suffocate
in their own innocent blood.

MARCHERS

the marching line is
out of step with the music
for the stars and stripes
not gently played. the
wealthy politicians put on
their masks before blinding
us with tear gas and they never
confess their acts of national
disgrace. the adversaries of duty
and the man calling truth
a lie fill the trusting ears of
citizens with the things that
lead them riotously astray,
and a staggering distance
from America's weariest, loudest
cries. these marchers are out
of step in their country led by
a fat politician who teaches his
pastors, judges, legislators, family,
and friends the ins and outs of hate
that mutes the nation's varied carols
and replace them with brand-name,
appalling ideas of "great."

FORGOTTEN HOUR

I open my eyes in the
dark, wakened by sounds
beyond the window from
a siren with lights wildly
flashing to push what is left
of night into the early hour
of a new day. I can see the
first bodies making their way
down the sidewalks for the
journeys they have packaged
the night before with beliefs
that followed them to this old
city from other shores. I saw
Magda walk by the window,
certain she carried in her bag
the pictures of her family living
on the Southside of this northern
continent. the scene outside this
tenement window will continue
to welcome images of people
rushing to work, children dashing
to school, stray dogs scavenging
food, and before the sun entirely
rises, the unremarkable migrants
who settled on this block, who
are faces without names to the
rest of the city. they will whisper
on the busses and subways, "Someday

the blindfolds will drop from the
eyes of people who think their country
is great and even kneel to pray in rich
churches.

1965

I remember the howling in
the tenement hallway when
in 1965 a blackout hit the city.
the Pentecostals in the building
came out with flashlights to
declare the beginning of the
end. I wondered whether that
meant we had to hide beneath
a kitchen table or go to a near
closest while taking a peek at
the sky for a look at what was
coming. it sure was dark and not
one perilous fire was devastating the
old buildings, meanwhile across the
alley, where Lefty, Shorty, and Lelo
lived, the guys were burning candles
and shouting like air-raid horns in open
space. phones were jammed, elevators
stalled, subways packed with people
were left in dark tunnels, the Cold
War between the US and USSR
popped into little kids' heads and
I sat in the dark with Papo talking
about *Dr. Strangelove* and nuclear
Armageddon. when I turned on an
old six transistor radio to hear the
country was not under attack, it was
like the cops just crashed the party

in Margarita's apartment just when
we were about to head up to the
roof to search for oddities in the
sky, mysterious fireballs, and—who
knew?—maybe even get a glimpse
of the Blackest God the world
would ever know, riding in on
a chariot, wearing sneakers made
of rubber and canvas with a cool
star on the side like the ones we
loved to wear every day until
it was time to dangle them from
the telephone wires still above
the ground on West Farms Road.

THE CLASSROOM

I sit with seminarians each week in
the passing hours of morning and
words trip off inquisitive tongues
about the spiritual things God-talk
suggests invisibly exist in all the
world. I question with them what
in the many marvels beneath the stars
is true and just what it is they read
or hear from the words I share that
is different from the White ideas
long inside their heads. before they
make it to the classroom in that dim
quiet space, I look around, recalling
days of studying in such a place the
story of God, the tree of knowledge,
good and evil locking heads in the
world, and America's original sin,
and then I wonder just what words
shared that day will be like dark flesh
for colleagues greeted in the halls and
the precious students who spend their
time behind these walls studying the
tales of creation's greatest love. as I
walk too blindly sometimes in life, God,
familiar with tortured flesh and the sins
causing premature death to the ethically
innocent, sometimes enters the seminary

classroom to declare Caesar will soon
weep on his imperial knees.

BLINK

theology, we can't stop
there, nor in the morning
thoughts of a professor
trained to declare the
mystery of heaven in
transitory flesh. candles,
on the altar of Saints
in the night trying to
trap with dancing light
a glimpse of the love
in the eternal mind so
lost by us. Hume, you
got it wrong—life is more
than mere sensations to
press into ideas and deeper
than what passes by many
names in metaphysics that
you will label a falsehood
of indigestion. death, you
only visit once and treat
us all the same, but even
you cannot foresee the
Holy room that waits nor
entirely measure your very
worthless sting. Calvary,
your costly secrets walk
each tangled day with us,
and when this finite sigh is

done, we will dissolve and
rise in marching time changed
into never-ending life.

THANKSGIVING

how do we give thanks for
history that passed rapidly
from plowshares to swords
when evil went around in circles
across the land, consuming the
children of God without European
names? where do we begin to speak
of hate carried by the wind from the
southern states to the mountains and
the lands of Black humanity kept for
centuries in chains? when was the last
time we cried in the shadows of night
for the women and children who crossed
the border river to rot in White jails? it
begins, holding up a lantern in the dark
and praying to end the malodorous ignorance
and silence that keeps a country from living
any wiser in the overvalued time of wholly
discredited love.

THANKS

we gave thanks today with
praises in the storefront church,
shouted at the top of our lungs
and perfectly timed to the sounds
of babbling infants. we gave praise
today, yelling "Amen!" whenever the
old preacher's speech gave us what
we did not have and told us with
a thousand words to look around
the room and give praise. we
prayed today with bellies full of
food for those who never listen,
la migra speaking mercifully in
Spanish, the rich who own the
banks, forests that are dying, and
the sun that gently warms us. we
rejoiced in the Spanish blessings
that reached us from your big
storehouse in the sky, for the
bits of English so far learned,
and the hands stretched out to
touch us with a welcome not
yet known. we bowed our heads
today around a table piled with
Mesoamerican treats to recall
the shacks so near to God and
the homes that now hold us up
with gracious love to make the

lost dreams of America sing in
many tongues of pity for the
loathed, elderly, vulnerable,
and poor.

THE STOOP

on the concrete steps of
the stoop just before you
enter the building, all the
names of the Brown boys,
painted in black, like jewels,
swept each day by the South
Bronx wind, longingly declare
in Spanish lives more precious
than the first feasts of Spring.
after school, Julio, still carrying
a backpack full of books, sat with
friends, asking them to hear, of all
things, Shakespeare's written speech
about the woes of strangers subject to
the barbarous temper and inhumanity
that makes a home by banishing the
weak. on the stoop, the Brown boys
kept spinning stories about school, cigar-
smoking abuelas, and the radio pumping
out fifties hits from a second-floor window
where Carmen the beautician happened to
live. these kids, with more than petty cares,
live with joy, and not a word of nativist speech
will hold them in its spell, nor keep them on the
other side of a Wall.

CLEANING DAY

it was one of those mornings
for cleaning the linoleum floor
with King Pine, with the wind
rattling the apartment window,
the voices in the hallway on the
other side of the door talking so
loud the dust on top of the black-
and-white television in the living
room was kicked into the air and
could be seen by the rays of light
creeping in. the afternoon plan was
to pray in the Spanglish church up
the street between two other mothers
with kids in public school learning to
read in English, and whisper gossip in
the dim sanctuary where the wounded
line up for communion. it was one of
those days for walking back to the old
apartment without words in the leftover
reality of Puerto Ricans living poor on
the block and to the fifth floor of the
building where a freshly cleaned floor
smelling of Pine-Sol escorted you into
an adorable room with an altar full of
clay Saints that somehow and in a very
mysterious way granted favors.

PSALM 46

there is a river flowing
to God's delight, like a
hyphen between nations.
come and see the Most High
who dwells in its trembling
waters, who gives refuge and
strength to the earth's meek and
brings to their desolate world
the sweetest peace. come to
wade in the water of the God
of the poor who shatters hate,
breaks policemen's batons, and
burns down the Walls erected by
the impenitent with fear. come to
the roaring river to see for yourself
the ultimate One, by whatever name,
that is our strength, even when it is
difficult to sing.

EXODUS

in the slowly moving time
of the year, in a period when
fewer people even in church
believe kindness matters on
earth like in heaven, migrants
walk from ancient lands in dark
night and risk crossing the river
again and again. I have tried to
use words beside the running
water to explain Pharaoh's newest
chariots rolling up and down
the border to slow the march
and say that as the river seeks
the sea you will find mothers,
brothers, sisters, uncles, aunts,
grandmothers, children, and new
English-speaking friends on the
other side, waiting with stories
of the grave of Jesus, empty. in
the slowly moving night, with
the wind gently pushing stained
blankets that bundle the thin bodies
of toddlers, I hear them confess
God, who touches tired Brown
bodies and waves a hand to clear
away the smell of mourning you
carry from other parts, and lets you

cross the border into a new land you,
like many, will not ever leave.

REST

It is already dark and
the street lights are
coming on. wearing
old hoodies with fading
words in yellow and red
they exit the bus at a stop
with a sign announcing the
newest fragrance of French
perfume. In the crowded
loneliness the mason brushes
his pants clean like a burden
lifted, and a little girl singing
runs into the bodega for the
last loaf of bread. they walk
with little left but hunger and
tears to give. tonight, walk
with me until we find a place
of surprising laughter.

EL MOZOTE

I walked a long way into
the field at the bottom of
the grassy hill to pray over
unmarked graves with the
women who still weep for
the civil war dead. there
were no stones with verse
in that place, the women
slowly shared memories
of their pain along with
special words about how the
church burned the day the
village died. we waited in
the silence for a sign, some
type of heavenly light to
overwhelm the dark into
which our eyes stared, even
for massacred children to
miraculously rise up and
resume their games. I saw
the dead these women felt
telling tales in the clean air
of this village the world does
not know exists, and where
these families bled for peace.
we prayed loudly to the God
who promised to rid the world
of sorrow.

KISSED

one evening in summer, I
recall hearing a voice in the
alley singing lullabies learned
in the coffee fields the twisted
Angels evaded. my mother at
the table in the kitchen, gluing
together costume jewelry for a
Jewish shop, looked at me and
smiled for the lonely singer that
never received applause. I learned
to listen that cool evening to the
old woman that made our hearts
pound with righteous messages that
poured from a beautiful Black soul
directly into us. when the moonlight
came into the apartments and the last
lullaby echoed against the old tenement
windows, restless Puerto Rican children
like me fell into the sleep that kept us
far away from the streets.

THIEVES

damn,
the law
ain't for
rich
White men
and women
who
never fall
down
and who
spin
the world
around,
piece
by
piece
with greed.
shit,
even God's
anger
is
lost in
their
felonious
world.
last I
heard,
they

haven't
read
a word
of
the
Bible
despite
the pious
faces
they
make.
we
should
let
them
wake
up in
a cheap
room,
broke,
before
any
more
poor
perish.

TRAVELERS

my father from Guatemala crossed
the border in Texas before the Second
World War when it had an open door.
he never called himself Hispanic, a
national minority, a wretched Indian,
a grade-school dropout, or a man with
mislaid memories of his ancient Mayan
land. he fought US-supported dictators,
fled a river of blood to exile, and said so
long to the pyramids found in the jungle
by those Spaniards who hunted Indians
with dogs. he walked across the border
into America, became a sailor for his new
country, fought for her in a world war,
slipped into death in a veteran's hospital,
and had his ashes scattered in the ocean
off a South American shore. mother, with
a Barcelonan father, is from Naguabo, PR
and a United States citizen since birth to
parents never married, that sang their sorrows
to a very distant Catholic God. when she
arrived in New York City, the East River
took bets on how many days of hunger
it would take to ruin her dreams. in the South
Bronx, she drifted into an aunt's house who
made a dime by making her a child bride to
an older guy that left tears in her eyes. her
soft bones gave birth to three kids in a

world of endless night until courage gave
her the heart to flee. in the thick
years of being beaten and tossed
she had a final breath in a hospice
bed trying to forget lost days and
holding fast to the idea that her eldest
son, turning to dust beneath Staten
Island earth, would meet her even in
the dimmest light at heaven's gate. this
man and woman were born, lived, and
died. believe me, I did not know them
well, suffered their mistakes, but love
them just the same.

THE PROJECTS

we always thought the projects
in the South Bronx were better
living than the old tenements
all the White folks fled the day
they heard Spanish in the halls,
after all, a Supreme Court justice
was raised in one of them. these
uniform warehouses the Puerto
Rican kids longed to live in did
not speak many languages, and
they hardly ever crossed the color
line, but they kept their residents
closer to the government and it
seemed living in them was a sure
answer to prayers. I can't tell you
how many times the single mothers
on the block kneeled in front of the
altar in Lela's apartment, having a
long conversation with the ceramic
figure of the Holy Mother about the
possibility of divine intervention to
get into one of those new buildings
that seemed closer to the promised
land. one lady sobbed through the
devotions, mumbling something about
cleaning bathrooms and wiping mirrors
in them downtown and even feeling too
poor to die. the candle burning on the

altar danced while other women in the room petitioned the Holy Mother to hear the cries, touch wounds, and get them into the damn projects! I sat with these single mothers in the altar room and listened to their prayers, but damn, we never got into the projects and America never stopped saying, "No matter where you live, be grateful, spics!"

ADVENT

in the store window
a nativity of animals,
an unwed mother, and
colors from the *barrio*
world are displayed.
pedestrians pause to
look and conjure up
a different world, to
shatter their darkest
fears and begin days
with God in heaven,
smiling on the earth.
in the rejoicing season
and all the mystifying
hours in church, even
people of other faiths
are split open by the
sign of overpowering
divine love.

THE SEASON

today, the infant in the
manger seeks children
in cages, flesh-and-blood
mothers hungry in cells,
old women who walked,
familiar with strife, and the
pitiable poor stretched out
flat in US camps. today,
children who cry hear the
Holy infant weep, while the
stench of the stable where the
Little One sleeps imperils Herod
in every age and place. today,
from the money-making jails,
words ascend to high heaven,
Spanish petitions learned from the
womb, demanding miracles on this
big earth, prayers uttered against the
terror felt by the wretched in these
scandalous times, words inviting the
heavenly choir to sing in earthly ears
and give light so all eyes see. today,
the bells loudly ring to declare the
great border crossing of a kind God
who leans into flesh to deliver good
news and blessings.

THE MANAGER

it's the end of the semester,
when the books have been
read and seminarians have
imagined places in need of
a visit with messages of some
kind of good news. a baker
in the classroom gives witness,
saving lives with bread that
never sins against the weak
nor denies a morsel to the
rich. we wonder together
in the advent season about
prayers lifted to heaven in the
name of an infant whose unwed
mother was denied room at an
inn. not a single Angel breaks
the silence to tell us where the
petitions go or how many languages
they speak. our hearts begin to sing
the seasonal hymns so relevant for
these sallow times, and just up the
street, in the dark alleys, the nameless
disregarded by the well-dressed confess
heaven sent a Prince of Peace who once
laid in a trough full of hay receiving
visits from three foreign kings. after all
the books, we turn the greatest page
to admit a single heartbeat of the infant

child in the worst of times can deliver
us to the simple joys of mercy,
justice, and love.

DOUBT

wandering out of the *barrio*,
I have prayed for many years
to become a Christian, though
you may find it a bit odd to
muse. I have scoured the pages
of the good book where truths to
believe are found, prayed for Tita's
youngest child to be raised from
the dust, and cried out to heaven
for hateful systems to end their
days. more than once have I called
upon the Lord, faltered on the
streets, looked for the slightest
beam of light, and questioned the
divine silence. I will not hesitate
to say Christians who have celebrated
faith in Christ by military conquest
and squeezing life out of the poor
have filled me with repugnance, and
the moral revulsion such piety invites
has made me vigorously pray for the
gates of hell to open wide and send
flames to burn away the lies pastors,
priests, and masquerading congregants
hold dear. I confess to having doubts
but they are not greater than the infinite
value of life, the good news descended
from heaven into an infant, the need to

love others on this crooked earth, and taking up the suffering of God in the world. I can tell you now that in this blessed religious season, I will weep with others who are in places kept out of sight and where God most certainly is found.

THE DISINHERITED

on this block, beneath
the brightest star below
heaven, the broken, hungry,
imprisoned, lost, and despised
live. the dark-skinned poor up
and down the grimy street
already feel the saving hand
that breaks all chains and rings
sweet bells around the earth to
call nations to the work of peace.
yes, night and day, we hear ringing
in our ears and the sublime carols
from worldly lips of second birth.
still, on some stoops of this old city,
people here and there cry, "Hate is much
too strong but louder still we will sing."
the God who cannot live without us is
leaning into history to grant the life
promised since the parting of the Red
Sea.

WINTER NIGHT

I crossed the street that
winter hunched over and
squinting in a strong wind
that carried swirling snow
to the sidewalks. I thought, "Only
two more blocks to Rockefeller
Plaza," where a very tall tree
stood looking over a court
and skating rink where people
wearing smiles from every borough
and other places on earth glided
on ice in thin light. I looked at
the tall tree and the many colored
upturned faces, wondering about
the voice that said let there be light
and how small the world must really
be to God. I closed my eyes, attending
to the hymn-singing shops, and the horns
furiously beeping on Fifth Avenue like
midtown lullabies. I saw people
leaving a Saint Patrick's Cathedral
Mass in silence, and then looked
around, trying to figure out where
to warmly sleep the night, and an
idea rushed me like a mugger on
the subway at 2 a.m. hope is the
noisy street with lost souls full
of life.

JOB

on the named streets of
this old city the churches
seldom love I see happy
faces of children that never
fade from life. on painted walls
of buildings I see tributes to
these streets, the twisted bones
of parents, the shacks on distant
shores, a Latinx rapper dead before
his time, a group of grandmothers
resurrected, and the Black face
of God sharing a divine breath
on a crowded sidewalk. on the
corners of the block, I see families
quietly waiting for the Lord to make
his rounds in places wrecked by hunger,
illness, poverty, prison, and death. on
the English-named streets, I see Brown
people counting blessings lived and yet
to come!

SIMPLICITY

every year a simple faith
is played by church bells
that awaken us to value
love, charity, and peace. on
corners till nightfall, you
hear them sing, "Never fear, the
bent Lord is near." even when
you think of it least the simple
sound is coming long before
you stand on the corner, sit on
a stoop, or in your apartment to
listen. every year the bells like
Angels' voices break into the
silence to slide us into the gentle
gifts that give themselves only
on these streets.

BRONX TALE

once, sitting late into
a brooding night, kids
began to spill dreams
when Mario told the
fast-moving Spanglish
tongues astrophysicist
Neil deGrasse Tyson
was born down here
and the Supreme Court
boricua now in DC
prefers being called
Sonia from the Bronx.
damn, you know who
else came from these
streets? Cardi B, Jennifer
Lopez, Willie Colon,
Bobby Sanabria, Chazz
Palminteri, Rob Reiner,
Cuba Gooding Jr., George
Carlin, Tracy Morgan,
Fat Joe, and even Tony
Curtis. the kids from
these spurned streets, used
by politicians like props,
cursed by the government,
battered by the cops, trashed
by public schools, and full
of dreams smiled at each other

more colorfully than the murals
they painted on walls.

LEGAL

they lived reaching across
borders in the dark, wading
rivers with dreams, resting
the nights caressed by the
wind and unafraid to cry in
each other's arms. they walked,
chatting in Spanish in the voices
of villages left behind and like
people eager to vent and give
testimony. often, they turned
like dust in the wind to avoid
detection on roads, took turns
reading out loud from a Bible,
and imagined calling across
miles from a dirt path into a
new American landscape ready
to have them light candles and
unpack a few precious things
carried in packs. they lived
in a world that called them
illegal, though each one of
them had names: Esperanza,
Sonia, Miguel, Ana, Angel,
Caridad, Maria, Jose, Juan,
son, daughter, mother, niece,
cousin, father, brother, uncle,
aunt—and each made legal
by God.

HATE

in the quietest room,
I sat with my daughter
last night, talking about the
loveliness of the blameless
Brown schoolgirl faces whose
names she said. she asked
out loud why a White woman
would drive her car down
a sidewalk to run down one
of them. afraid of her own
country, I watched tears rolling
down her cheeks for all the
sweet girls with dark-colored
skin mowed down by hate on
American streets. I wrapped
my arms around her, saying, "Don't
be afraid. There are hearts that
have love left in them to sing,
and our ancient souls will never
be lacerated by this White hate
that God abhors, especially when
they proudly laugh whenever we
take a knee to grieve."

TRENZAS

each year the mail
carrier arrived early
on the first floor of
the building to sort
letters in boxes with
rusted locks. never
was there a card in
his bundle with wise
men and shepherds
following a star or
weary barn animals
gathered around an
infant God. on this odd
hallmark land, when
they ask what it was like
not to get a Christmas
card, I say, "The Brown
abuela hands so practiced
at kneading corn never
did learn to write." when
they ask how does that
feel, I say, "We simply lit
a candle and uttered
weighty prayers that
made their way into a
southern land across the
border and whispered
into *abuela* ears: we

will press another rose
in the pages of the Bible,
everyone will say your name
and pass the braided hair picture
of you around on Christmas
morning—you know, the one
we carried over three thousand
miles in a sack, with you wearing
beautiful long hair in *trenzas* older
than America!"

MIGRANT MOTHERS

the apartment only had
three rooms ,though it was
known for being a guest
house for mothers with
children. they waited years
to make the long journey,
share what violent men did
to them and walk the streets
of hell to live. they prayed
for weeks for other mothers
behind bars denied medicine,
water, kindness and separated
from their innocent kids caged
somewhere else. the mothers
with children who make it to
the guest house on the street of
this old city arrive, because for
them God is escaping to a new
life, wiping away the beatings,
believing in a future closer than
thousands of miles away, and singing
lullabies to Brown-skinned kids with
Spanish names and talkative tongues
for ages to come.

THE ROAD

I am encircled by displaced
people God sees in a world
that doesn't feast with strangers
and believes bread is not given
from above for the good of one
another on earth. I miss walks
on mountains through the clouds,
the winding river flowing down
hillsides rinsing them clean, the
night beneath the stars I was taken
by the hand by a nameless child to
a Ceiba tree with names carved into
its massive trunk, and yelling with
friends where the forest bent into
secrets then waiting for answers to
rush out from trees. I miss the
trick of light in the distant valley,
the sound of Spanish on the streets
and the days that tirelessly carried
us from childhood. I wrapped these
memories in my heart and look at
them on dark nights when they offer
light in forbidden English cities that
sometimes make me wander too far
from my people.

BLESSING

a woman crosses the street,
holding her daughter's hand,
her complicated eyes looking
north and south. out of habit
on a free day from work, she
is on the way to the boulevard
with shops after kneeling in a
church where she let things go
and prayed for them to forget
how to build walls. with her little
girl, she will walk the very long
street in search of a moment of
extravagant delight on the Spanish-
speaking sidewalk and tomorrow's
prayers will be made from it. she
will pause in the little park by the
highway where her daughter will
run freely and there recall the day
she gave thanks after crossing miles
of desert and seeing flowers bloom
in sand.

THE CAMPS

when we enter the brick church
we tell whomever is listening that
we have been fleeing a country
that put a price on our heads. for
years the executioners have been
paid in dollars. first soldiers came,
full of nocturnal villainy, trained in
Georgia to skin us alive, and then the
gangs born in East LA started running
the streets and the women selling bread
were their first violent feast. our Brown
faces with tearing eyes that have gathered
round cheap wood coffins nearly every day
have walked a long way to the country that
blew up an Alabama church with four Black
girls inside in prayer. we only go to Mass
to weep for the mothers in camps, children
with numbers on their arms driven off to
jail, the suffocating prisons with people
pressed like cattle into too-small rooms
and a country barely leaning toward the
light. when you finally come looking for
us in American concentration camps
after eating the substance of God in
your pretty churches, do not act surprised
to find nothing of us but dry bones and
mounds of dust.

BARBARISM

I went to schools where
truth was broken into bits,
dressed with nauseating lies,
and taught God in heaven
guided a murderer, slaver,
and European thief named
Columbus across the sea to
start colonial tyranny. I sat
in classrooms that never said
a word about de las Casas's *The
History of the Indies*, filled
with stories that made his
Christian hand tremble, writing
of barbarism and inhumanity
unlike any had ever seen. the man
so many teachers repeated set
out to prove the world was not
flat had himself to admit what
the West buried deep there was
a Black presence in the West
before the slave trader from
Italy set foot on Hispaniola.
you who teach heroizing White
myths, remember this historical
fact: Black and Brown humanity
in the Americas began their lives
free!

END OF A YEAR

the calendar lies naked on the
last day of the parting year and
it has us thinking about what was
done and left to wander to some
place where no Bethlehem Star is
lighting a way. laughter, tears,
vows, fresh flowers on tables, and
cups lifted will see us trip into the
new year, and in this beginning of
time again, with all that we know,
everything looks possible. perhaps
we will listen more closely to the
shouting in the darkness and see
the reservoir of dreams spray-painted
on the walls of buildings by inner-city
kids whose names the three wise
men remember. perhaps we will learn
to breathe for the infants who start
their days in a jail cell, the children
with numbers on their arms, the
Spanish-speaking mothers twisted
by sadness, and the beautiful toasted
people who see the sunrise and feel
the morning breeze, unable to know
delicious joy. perhaps the wrong
roads will be left behind in the old
year and the days, weeks, and months

to come will be less mad and far too beautiful even for heartaches.

NEVER FORGETTING

your mother knew the
martyrs that shed tears
by telling the world facts
about the fatal divisions
not ordained by God. she
files into church in the mornings
to pray with them, makes her
way to the altar to light a few
candles, directing earth to be
more like heaven, and weeps
about the American money
sent to make thousands of
martyrs on village streets
in the name of some White
Protestant Christianity. she
started the new year again in
church, chanting the names of
those without gravestones and
families who still believe though
they are locked in White House
cells. I will sit with her on the
other side of darkness, gazing
on the sacred text carefully placed
beneath a cross in the cathedral
visited by the poor. I will keep
one eye open while she says the
rosary to catch, with a little luck,
sight of grieving Angels who will

caress our broken hearts, explain
God's numerous mistakes, and give
us good news from the man whose
body was nailed to a tree.

SNOWY NIGHT

the stores on Southern Boulevard
began to close while snow gently
drifted down from the sky to brush
lightly across the sidewalk and then
settle. soon, foot patterns could be
seen heading in every direction and
signs of the running feet of children
invited you to their playful shouting
voices on a distant corner. white
flakes poured from the darkening
sky, rising after a few hours to the
height of the curb at the subway
station on Simpson Street, and life
at the edges of the city could not be
more complete. in the air, the whirling
snowflakes were never two alike, floating
down from heaven and looking more
beautiful than frail in the expanding
South Bronx night. it would not be
long for them to end their flight and
heap together in a quiet spot just like
the people piled in the apartments worn
out by the complicated details of their
undocumented lives. tonight, speech
lends itself to stories, and with them
the people in the crowded room will
drift to Spanish lands more precious
than the falling snow.

THE *ABUELITA*

the *abuelita* in the apartment
across the hall is always dressed
in black, with a Spanish lace scarf
worn on her head. neighborhood
kids on the way to school most
mornings can see her at the fire
escape window, watering an herb
box the landlord tolerates despite
the inspector's warnings. she lives
in a three-room apartment with her
grandson, who understands the
Spanish words that pour from her
lips though he only speaks a few
of them himself and sometimes
just opens an empty mouth making
believe a whole Spanish sentence
is about to run out. when you walk
by her apartment door you sometimes
stop to listen to music scattering Puerto
Rican words in songs never heard on
the street or radio. we think the old
woman is the most fragile member of
the block, the first one to make history
in the city, open school doors, tell local
White priests to defend the poor and sit
on the stoop, grinning until dawn, sharing
exquisite stories older than the tropical
nights that live in her soul.

THE CROSSING

God, you crossed the
border from heaven to
enter human flesh and
cry with an infant face
in the stench of a stable.
God, your tired teen mother
held you in her arms and whispered
the first sweet words that let
you drift into sleep. God, what
did Maria say? will she tell
us stories about you when a
poor child? God, you enchanting
undocumented stranger, why did
you stop touring the stars to find
a place with us? Maria, will you tell us
before the infant grows and departs,
pinned to a tree, what foolishness
from heaven will liven trust in us
to carry us to the end of time and
swiftly across the sweet Jordan
river?

THE BEGGAR

asleep on the church steps
he dreamed of the East River,
flowing down the avenue with
beer bottles wrapped in brown
paper bags with words written
in magic marker he could not
make out. the night was around
him and the windows, slightly open
in the apartments across the street,
were singing a thousand versions
of the same song found in the old
prayer book of the church where
Mass in Spanish was said in a cold
basement. for the last three years
he stopped praying with the people
in the neighborhood always asking
for heavenly favors and spends each
day spreading the gospel like a beggar
on the street who lives nights on the
pitiless church steps.

MEMO FROM GOD

it took him many years
to realize difference was
spreading faster than the
editorials penned by the
learned men lacking the
basic intelligence to say
foreign-sounding names.
the books resting on his
bedroom desk never told
stories about the kids shot
by scheming cops, money-
loving preachers with words
for beating spics, and the bloody
rich politicians cursing by the
hour the dark hands that will
build the monuments that record
their accomplished hate. it took him a
long time to realize the good White
Lord he dreamed who never lost
a drop of light hanging on a filthy
old tree did not understand English
words used to satisfy the heresy
of people who never traveled by
foot from far, or looked into a
colored face to see the perfect
image of God!

THE SIRENS

when we heard the sirens at
2 a.m. no one believed it was
Rudy who didn't make it until
sunlight. we listened to the noise
behind the triple-locked apartment
door where only a few hours earlier
we feel asleep hungry. sometimes the
streets were beautiful and for little
kids always made a whole lot of good
sense. we could not remember how
many times old women on the block
spoke crossly about the privileged
White folk on the other side of the
Bronx who did not believe *barrio* boys
like Rudy were the salt of the earth.
they found him on the Holy darkness
of the sidewalk: just another wretched
Puerto Rican no longer breathing,
threatening to darken up America's
days. the knock at the door came from
a White cop and before finishing his
sentence I tightened up, trying to hold
back tears, and understood the meaning
of being a spic who labors for others'
gain with a name insignificant, like
a speck of dust on the barren street
that finally settled my brother's last
thought. Shit, dead at thirty-one!

DISJOINTED

I did not find God stepping into
church in any of the pretty voices
of the Methodist choir. I listened
in the dim sanctuary and admit the
singing lifted me above the earthly
darkness and darn close to the very
spot where I imagine the Lord must
have stood the day he hurled creation
into its various unmanageable parts.
I did find traces of divinity in living
things like dogs in the alley, old men
with beer cans in brown paper bags
impatient widows waiting to be seen
at a social security office, buried in the
face of adolescents shooting dope on
a roof, winos hustling hotdogs from
carts on Fifth Avenue, and sitting
sometimes in that church, speaking
Spanish. this may sound crazy but I
heard God singing last Sunday when
city lights at last turned off and only
stars brightened night, but not a word of
paradise was carried by the tune. I think
it strange that those threatened with death
will arrive again next week once again
to hear wounded European hymns.

EARTHQUAKE

the wind swallowed up
the shores just a few years
ago and now the earth
rattled the dark depths
of Puerto Rican souls to
shed more tears on land
colonially enslaved and
for centuries by rich White
men lynched. standing on
the cracked earth today, it
is clear liberty for citizens
on this rock in the middle of
the sea is fictitious thought
and a grave social ill. Lord,
forbid harm to this enchanted
place, listen closely to your
people in prayer, their delicious
words asking for more life, and
mercifully join them in days to
come in any village songs and
dances that will beat back sorrow
and pain.

THE BULB

the light in the hallway of the
building is like a mystery that
lures apartment-dwellers to the
excesses of the Most High that
the most recent arrivals from
El Salvador insist is present,
like water made into wine at the
wedding in Cana. I never cared too
much for that kind of old-country
talk, especially when the cries in
the alleys, the rooftops, and lavish
cathedral never resulted in loving
caresses from God and the things
to save could be seen on the block
like flowers in suburban gardens. I
was the foolish kid asking a thousand
questions about the haunting silence
of the gods and their apparent deafness
to the sounds of spics. I do confess, my
sweet darling, I have changed my mind
over the years, but with my gray hairs
telling their own stories, I cannot tell you
in this bruising world with a flaming
tongue quite how.

THE INVENTION

they invented heroin abuse
on Hoe Avenue during the
Vietnam War and brand-
named street dope enjoyed
Brown bodies far more than
Jesus visited them. I can tell
you Hector was not ruined by
drink; just a thick old needle
that made daily rounds in his
veins, walked him into a cold
prison cell and without a single
scream laid him calmly to rest in an
unforgiving grave. I suppose some
people living White would say this
son of a failed mother was finally
cured. I never heard him thank God
for being a junkie pioneer in New York
City, nor within the context of his habit
say the sidewalk beneath his feet where
the Pentecostals often stood to pray was
holy ground. Hector simply departed
as the world slept and the only thing left
of him is an incident report written in
English no one reads.

CAMP HERESY

you have children in camps
with numbers on their tiny
arms darker than your God
and unable to speak a word
of English just like Jesus. you
might not notice but these little
kids know how to kneel in cold
cells and pray to the blackness
that does not hold any hate for
them. I dare you to make a visit
with your best translator one day
to learn the name of each one of
them and enjoy the moment more
than a proverbial slice of Thanksgiving
Day American pie! I dare you to walk
away from a numbered child's cage and not
confess those who put them in it only believe
Christ hangs on the cross just to smell his armpits!

MOUNTAINTOP

it is time again to say in
every outspoken prayer
the near-perfect dreams
helping us cross into other
worlds. it is time again to
visit the mountaintop above
the hideous places to see a
new world for earth and fill
our mouths with words for
the first time ever heard. it is
time to throw stones at pulpits
looking away from the world
with carefully crafted lies to
conjure confederate visions
of America and blazing immigrant
hate. it is time to confess in this
season of discontent that proves
nightmares true, "God, in pity, will
wake us up soon!"

WHIRLWIND

there are no grandiose cathedrals
dotting the streets in this city with
mysteries. the mournful widows
who soak their pillows each dark
night come to sit on the steps of
the only temple left open to them
on the block. children who play
on the streets still tell what they
recall of vanishing Spanish tales
heard on magical summer nights
in a language shrewdly abducted
by public schools and television
shows from their tongues. we often
complain to *La Virgen,* who answers
to different names, about our rooms
without Angels, the low-flying police
helicopters frightening the pigeons on
the roof, and how in America pain is
carried by the dark-skinned. there are
no secrets on either side of the river
to keep the world from hearing about
the latest lynching, no pages to tear
out of the press to forget, no churchy
words in English or Spanish to scour the
pious clean of their terminal complicity
in assassinating with worthless theology
the disappearing people who are not loved.

IMPEACH

we have not gone a day
without our minds fixed
on the newest American
politics made by the draft-
dodging, thoughtless, and
unread-world-alarm man in
the White House protected
by White privilege. we have
not made sense of this failed
politician, his nationalist hate,
cruelty to spare, impulses to
war, and that outright insanity
that makes us weak. we do
not understand how a career
criminal, created in the image
of hell, spilling shit for words
and slaughtering public policy,
got elected and has so many
Senate friends to help him break
the law. we have memorized
his foul-smelling America and
it is not great!

NORTHERN CITY

I crossed to another city,
searching for the one talked
up in scripture, and went to
live on a block with all the
unknown people favored by
God. the old city took us in,
gave us places to sleep, was
kind to our children, always
offered balm for our blistered
hands, and at night yawned in
all the colors of our skin. many
say this place is nothing like the
heavenly city yet we walk on divine
streets, sing praises in storefront
churches, stand beneath the bright
streetlights, speaking Spanish with
words that laugh and every window
the way I remember it on this part
of town shouts using heaven's own
mysterious words to say Jesus will
be a little late.

REMEMBER

in the sixties, the old block
is where everybody danced the
pearl to Motown tunes, dressed
with Delancey Street ten-percent
silk vines, and invented Spanglish
slang on stoops. remember the news
rushing us in 1968 the day Martin
was killed, fires burned in Harlem,
the *Barrio*, the South Bronx, the Lower
East Side, and wailing spilled from
the doors of apartments into the
halls? remember how they called
us "colored" and "spics," sitting on the
porches of their suburban homes,
joking about the death of Martin,
Malcolm, John, and Robert? I bet
you never forgot the night in the
storefront church when the preacher
blessed us in broken English, raising
Black hands to say, "God, exile people
wadding in a shallow river, whistling
Dixie and reciting ten-cent prayers
with confidence." man, I know it feels
like nothing has changed, but let me
tell you not even a thousand murderous
blows can keep us from singing: "We
Shall Overcome! We shall be free!"

GUATEMALAN BOY

a sixteen-year-old boy from
Guatemala was thrown
sick into a small holding
cell by the Border Patrol
in South Texas. there is a
tape that shows him sinking
into the Whiteness of hate at
an overcrowded processing
showroom in McAllen, Texas,
while running a fever of 103
degrees, being transferred to a
nearby town cell, and in the shadow
of centuries of racist approval he
died. the boy never hurt a White
soul and not a word of perfectly
crafted prayer by ethically minded
church folk will bring this Brown
boy back from the dead nor change
the hearts of grown White men who,
grinning, said, "Die motherfucker!"
his death does not even live in the
memory of Christian America that is
too busy with the churchy explanations
that steer good people away from the
truth that still gets nailed to the Jesus
tree.

THE SEWER

tonight, I sit beneath a grey
sky far from the tavern in an
eastern city where people stop
on winter nights to rest enough
to change their faces and dry
their misty eyes. I think of the
uncertain lives weathering the
crisis of democracy, the madness
of the collection of politicians who
do evil to the helpless, the celebrity
attorneys with anemic morals and
mouths thick with lies. tonight, I
wonder who else is feeling angry
about the arc of history not leaning
toward justice and the elated dream
of the Republic driven away. tonight,
I listen to chatter from the Senate that
the perfect tyrant in the White House
has done nothing wrong, just like he
never stole from charities, did favors
for global dictators, paid hush money
to porn stars, worked to make Russia
great, put numbers on the arms of Brown
children sent to his camps, and got caught
extorting a foreign president for nothing
but self-gain. Tonight, I think of the poor
dying on the border, on American streets,
and democracy, with a whole lot of

unrespectable senators digging a
grave to honor the perfect madness
of the man who leads them through
the sewers of the nation to the money-
laundering banks. Shit, the outlaws
appear to run the government and
keep their favorite citizens deaf, blind,
and dumb!

PRAYER

Lord, can you hear
in heaven the shouts
from earth? Do you
have any time left to
gather up the meek,
the poor, the victims
of the vicious rich?
Crucified carpenter
from Galilee, do have
mercy on us! Come into
the darkness where we
live to offer gracious light,
a kiss, and delicious good
news!

WITNESS

pray loudly, *campesina*
mothers in your beautiful,
sunmade, Brown skin. pray
from the *barrio* rooftops so
heaven hears, use words to
split darkness in this weary
land, to lift up the desperate
and gather up the children the
good Lord occasionally forgets
to love. pray loudly when you
look down the forsaken streets,
take the neighborhood by hand
to purge each heart of sadness,
and whisper to the brokenhearted,
"The Lord's chariots are right around
the corner with Jesus, who will soon
be here, slapping a tambourine, and
shouting, 'Blessed are the meek!'"

HOLD ON!

when we left the church no
one with their bowed heads
believed God did not know
the troubles to come and the
ugly loads to carry while the
redneck's white hands slap us
down. the old lady with dark
skin was sitting on the church
steps selling prayer cards with an
image of *La Virgen de Guadalupe*
everyone knows doesn't speak a
lick of English, and thanks to the old
woman, no one doubted on the way
to Hunts Point that, come nightfall,
sleep would be full of dreams not
for sale. we walked with a spirit of
prayer, listening to the cries in the wind
chased by hate that entered the *barrio*
from pious places out of town where
people spend hours asking God to
kick us out! every step we took on
the way to the little park to watch
Black and Brown children play said we
didn't need the Lord's prayer, full stomachs,
and a job next week, when right now we
are pushed into graves. we talked into the
late afternoon, questioning, "Does the church
still own the word 'peace,' and does America

know anything now of freedom, justice, and equality?"

WAKE

here on the Lower East Side,
we settled too far back to
remember marking time by
the rising prices of things
in the bodega and the latest
layoff at work. on the rooftops,
we look over the rest of the
city, with our Spanish eyes
drifting to the Upper East
Side, where spics are prohibited
to live, just to marvel. the laws
have changed for strangers and
even though most of us are
citizens who pay the same fare
on the bus there are never too
few White folks on them thinking
you don't belong! on Sunday, we
get dressed in the only pair of fancy
clothes bought cheap on Delancey
Street, wrapped like apartment furniture
in plastic and kept in a closet for Jesus'
day. on Sunday, you will never see a
bigger line just to light a tiny candle
in the dark and hope words float out
the church door right to heaven from
our heartbreaking world.

MERCY

don't know why, Lord,
you put me to work with
no papers and said, "Don't
be afraid." don't know what
time of day you said I'd be
saved and I can't tell for sure
who crossed the desert and
came all this way not to see
your face. but listen, Lord,
have mercy on a poor old Brown
man, full of old-fashioned sin in
an English-speaking world, like me.

INFANTERIA BOULEVARD

God knows I never
thought the day would
come that a whole strip
of Southern Boulevard
would be named to honor
the Puerto Rican regiment
based on the island and
known in two world wars
and the Korea campaign as
the Borinqueneers. more
than twenty-thousand Puerto
Ricans served in the 65th
infantry, giving their lives
in service to the country
that calls them spics. the
imprudent 45th president
of the United States does
not even know islanders
like them gave America its
birth by sacrificing their lives
in the American Revolution,
alongside Cubans and, yes,
Mexicans, to fight the British
in 1779, while led by a Spanish
General known by the name
Bernado Galvez. you know,
since the American Revolution
Congress commissioned Gold

Medals as the highest expression
of national contributions and deep
appreciation. George Washington
received it, 158 others did too, and
few combat units. it took a Black
president to sign into law on June
14, 2014, bills H.R. 1726 and S.1174
to award the Congressional Gold
Medal to the 65th regiment or *el
sesenta y cinco de infantería!*—say
it loud with me. the career criminal
in the White House who tossed paper
towels to hurricane victims in a San
Juan relief center is one American
among many other tone-deaf assholes
that soldiers like the Borinqueneers
fought for to keep them talking shit
and free.

HOLLER!

the Mother of God sheds
tears older than the finest
church creeds for sanctuary
cities, caring for strangers
despised by a president
who subjects them to sniper-
certified tactical border
squads. God in heaven,
Shakespeare, the English
author these White nationalists
will never read, wrote, "hell
is empty and all of the devils
are here." when Brown folks
cross the river and over the
Wall, military units are called
to crush new American dreams
and the nation is less free! yes,
"O beautiful for spacious skies,
cops for Black lives that do
not matter, and Border Patrol
SWAT to make America great
by beating down Brown-skinned
Mesoamericans." mother of God,
crying with the poor, tell us, as they
take us to prison, when your crucified
son will make thousands of houses of
worship feel disgrace for not hollering
at this wrong.

THE MAN

it was yesterday, the
the single-page letter
never came, my Brown-
born body was shaking
in the overcrowded jail.
it made me wish all day
I never imagined heaven
could be found on a dark
piece of English-speaking
earth. it was yesterday, the
tragic prayers were said in
brightly lighted rooms with
mostly empty pews and the
muted voices still said nothing
of the terror coming from the
man who, without rope or tree,
lynches us with free speech
tweets.

HERE

the simple time opened
with a candle ingeniously
placed on the stoop where
not a single person who had
gathered with a heart full of
pious questions felt disabling
sorrow. no one claimed the
privilege to make a lengthy
speech that night about the
simple promises of heaven
not coming true. the burning
candle in the warm night had its
way of offering mysterious gifts
that words could never say. we
sat, turning the moments over with
laughter, holding them like a lover by
the hand, bribing them to never end.

THE CHILDREN

these days will never be
forgotten, their tiny hands
shivering in prison, their
dark bodies burdened with
strife, and their deaths farther
still from paradise. we will
never forget the lousy cages
of White fear where children
bled and gasped for air while
hateful preachers, politicians,
judges, and guards clapped and
laughed. the day will come for
cruelty to end and the words
for all we have lost will leave
our lips with the deeply buried
darkness. the day will come and
we will see these kids again in
heaven, running, laughing, and
hollering in sweet Spanish with
Angels who play.

www.ingramcontent.com/pod-product-compliance
Lightning Source LLC
Chambersburg PA
CBHW071420160426
43195CB00013B/1754